TWO WAYS OF PRAYING

TWO WAYS OF PRAYING

Introducing liturgical spirituality

Paul F. Bradshaw

OSL PUBLICATIONS
Maryville, Tennessee

Two Ways of Praying

Copyright 2008 by Paul F. Bradshaw

ISBN 978-1-878009-59-3

Produced and manufactured in the United States of America by
OSL Publications
the publishing ministry of The Order of Saint Luke
P O Box 5506
Maryville Tennessee 37801

Scripture quotations are from the New Revised Standard Version of the Bible, © 1989 by the Division of Christian Education of the National Council of the Churches of Christ in the USA. Used by permission.

Unless otherwise noted, quotations from writings of the early church are the author's translation.

The Order of Saint Luke is a religious order in The United Methodist Church, dedicated to sacrametnal and liturgical scholarship, education and practice. The purpose of the publishing ministry is to put into the hands of students and practitioners resources which have theological, historical, ecumenical and practical integrity.
www.saint-luke.org

This book is dedicated to the congregations among whom
I have had the privilege of serving
and who have taught me the meaning of prayer.

Contents

Preface

It may come as something of a surprise to some readers to hear that there are at least two ways of praying—with different concepts of what prayer itself is. So dominant has one particular spirituality become in nearly all Christian traditions today that many people are completely unaware that there might be such a thing as a *liturgical* spirituality or another way of understanding or organizing their worship and prayer life. This book has been written, therefore, primarily to open up that other way of praying to a wider audience and show that what it has to offer is an important complement to the understanding of prayer with which Christians are generally familiar.

Much of the material in it has formed the basis for classes that I have taught and talks and workshops that I have given over the course of many years. Some of it has already appeared in quite different forms in articles I have written, and this is indicated among the "Suggestions for Further Reading" at the end of each chapter. Above all, it emerges at least as much out of the experience of my own prayer life as it does out of my scholarship, and so I pass it on in the sincere hope that it may prove as enriching to the spirituality of others as it has for me.

Paul F. Bradshaw
Christmas 1993

Preface to the Second Edition

The need for a reprint of this book has given me the welcome opportunity to make a few small corrections and to update the suggestions for further reading.

Paul F. Bradshaw
June 2007

1

"CATHEDRAL" AND "MONASTIC" PRAYER

Most people have at least a vague idea of what it is that they think that they are supposed to be doing when they are asked to engage in private prayer, but they are often much less clear about prayer in the context of public worship. Is this simply a collective version of individual prayer, or is it meant to be a quite different sort of activity? And what are they to make of suggestions that they should try to incorporate some elements from church services into their own daily prayers? Is this confusing two ways of praying? Or is the really important distinction not between public and private worship at all but between two different concepts of what it is that we are doing when we pray?

It is here that a look back at the history of Christian praying, and especially the practice of the early church, may prove illuminating. In studying the daily worship of fourth-century Christians, scholars often like to draw a distinction between what they call "cathedral" and "monastic" types of prayer, although in reality the situation was much more complex than that. There was, for example, an important difference between the worship of monastic communities in desert regions far away from parochial life and those in more urban settings closely associated with the ecclesiastical world around them. But for our present purposes, we may reasonably lay these historical subtleties to one side and concentrate instead on the broad outlines.

"Cathedral" and "monastic" are not particularly appropriate designations for these two types of prayer, because they can seem to suggest that "cathedral" worship only went on in cathedrals and that monastic communities always engaged in "monastic" prayer. This is far from the case. But because they have become accepted technical terms, we will continue to use them here. The distinction between the two ways of praying is not based primarily on the place in which the worship was offered, but rather on the variations in external forms of that worship, and more importantly on the significant differences of the inner spirit and understanding of prayer expressed by those divergent forms. Such a distinction, however, has a much wider application. These two different concepts of the nature of prayer are not just features of the fourth-century church but can be found throughout Christian history and thus have an important part to play in our understanding of prayer today. But first, let us take a look at two examples of "cathedral" and "monastic" prayer in their classical, fourth-century, context.

"CATHEDRAL" PRAYER

We are fortunate in having a quite detailed description of a "cathedral" style of prayer in part of a travel diary written by a pilgrim who visited Jerusalem in the last quarter of the fourth century. She appears to have been a nun named Egeria from western France or Spain who wanted to provide an account of what she saw for the other members of her religious community back home. Although the worship at Jerusalem was not entirely typical of other fourth-century centers of Christianity, and although our visitor may not have been accurate in every detail of her description, even so her account will suffice to convey the general spirit of "cathedral" prayer:

> So that your affection may know what services are held every
> day in the holy places, I must tell you, knowing that you would
> willingly wish to learn this. Every day before cockcrow all the
> doors of the Anastasis [the Church of the Resurrection] are
> opened, and the *monazontes* [monks] and *parthenae* [nuns],
> as they call them here, all enter, and not only these but also lay
> men and women besides who wish to keep an earlier vigil.
> From that time until dawn hymns are recited and psalms with
> their refrains, and antiphons too. . . .

When it begins to get light, then they begin to recite the morning hymns. Then the bishop comes with his clergy and immediately enters the cave, and from inside the screen he first recites the prayer for all, and he himself commemorates any names he wishes; then he blesses the catechumens. He recites another prayer and blesses the faithful. After this, the bishop comes outside the screen, and all come to his hand, and he blesses them one by one as he comes out, and so the dismissal takes place when it is already light.

Likewise at the sixth hour all again enter the Anastasis, and psalms and antiphons are recited while the bishop is sent for; and again he enters, and does not sit, but immediately goes inside the screen in the Anastasis—that is, the cave where he went earlier—and from there he again first recites a prayer; he then blesses the faithful, and comes outside the screen, and again they come to his hand. The ninth hour is the same as the sixth hour.

At the tenth hour—what they call here *Lychnikon* but we call *Lucernare*—all the people gather again in the Anastasis, and the lamps and candles are all lit, and the light is very bright. The light is not brought from outside, but is taken from inside the cave, that is, from inside the screen, where a lamp is always burning night and day. The *Lucernare* psalms and antiphons are recited for some time. Then the bishop is sent for, and he enters and takes his seat, and the presbyters also sit in their places. Hymns and antiphons are recited. When they have finished them according to their custom, the bishop rises and stands in front of the screen—that is, the cave— and one of the deacons makes the commemoration of individuals according to the custom, and when the deacon says the names of individuals, a large group of boys always respond, *Kyrie eleison*, or as we say, "Lord, have mercy." Their voices are very loud. When the deacon has finished all that he has to say, the bishop first recites a prayer and prays for all. So far the faithful and catechumens pray together. Now the deacon bids all the catechumens to stand where they are and bow their heads, and the bishop then recites the blessing over the catechumens from his place. There is another prayer, and again the deacon bids all the faithful to stand and bow their heads. The bishop then blesses the faithful, and so the dismissal takes place at the Anastasis, and individuals come to his hand (*Itinerarium Egeriae* 24).

"Monastic" Prayer

At about the same time as Egeria was visiting Jerusalem, a monk by the name of John Cassian was observing monastic practices in Egypt, where the monastic movement was born. He later settled in Gaul, and there he wrote a description of Egyptian monasticism for the benefit of the local religious communities. Although again the details of his account may not be historically reliable (in particular, he appears to have mingled together the practices of Upper Egypt with the somewhat different customs of Lower Egypt), yet he manages to capture the essentials of the ideal spirit of their daily devotions:

> Therefore, as we have said, throughout the whole of Egypt and the Thebaid the number of psalms is fixed at twelve in both the evening and the nocturnal celebrations, and two readings follow, one from the Old Testament and one from the New. . . .

> These aforesaid prayers, therefore, they begin and end in such a way that, when the psalm is over, they do not immediately hasten to kneel down, as some of us do in this country. . . . Among them, then, it is not so, but before they bend their knees, they pray for a while, and spend the greater part of the time standing for prayer. And so after this, they prostrate themselves on the ground for the shortest space of time, as if adoring the divine mercy, and rise up as quickly as possible, and again standing up with their hands outstretched in the same manner as they had prayed standing before, they prolong their prayers. . . . But when he who is to "collect" the prayer rises from the ground, they all get up at the same time, so that no one may presume to bend the knee before he bows down, nor to delay when he has risen from the ground, lest it should be imagined that he has not followed the conclusion of the one who "collected" the prayer but offered his own. . . .

> When, therefore, they gather to celebrate the aforesaid rites, which they call *synaxes*, they are all so silent that, although such a large number of brethren is assembled together, one

would think that nobody at all was there except the one standing up in the middle to chant the psalm, and especially when the prayer is completed, for then there is no spitting, no clearing of the throat, no noise of coughing, no sleepy yawning with open mouths and gasping, no groans or sighs to distract those around, and no voice is heard except that of the priest concluding the prayer. . . .

Therefore, they do not try to complete the psalms which they sing in the assembly with continuous recitation, but they divide them into two or three sections, according to the number of verses, with prayers in between, and work through them bit by bit. For they do not care about the quantity of verses, but about the intelligence of the mind, adhering strongly to this: "I will sing with the spirit; I will sing also with the mind." And so they think it better for ten verses to be sung with thoughtful understanding than for a whole psalm to be poured forth with a bewildered mind... (*Institutes* II: 4, 7, 10, 11).

CONTRASTS

As these two accounts suggest, some sharp contrasts between "cathedral" and "monastic" types of prayer can be noted. Five such differences are described here, although these and other contrasts will be explored more fully in subsequent chapters.

First of all, "cathedral" prayer is something that the whole congregation does. They sing the hymns and psalms together as an expression of their corporate praise. Even though an individual cantor might chant the actual verses, the congregation responds to each one with a refrain. Similarly, the intercessions which follow are an expression of their common concerns. At least at the evening hour in Egeria's description, each petition that is announced by the deacon is greeted with a congregational response, as the people make it their own. Worship is thus essentially communal—or rather ecclesial; for this is not just a prayer group, it is the church at prayer.

"Monastic" prayer, on the other hand, is fundamentally an individual activity. Although it may appear to be communal from Cassian's account, in reality there was nothing inherently corporate about it, nothing that absolutely required the presence of others, nothing that might not be done equally as well alone as together. Indeed, while the custom in Upper Egypt was for the community to meet together twice every day to pray, as Cassian's description claims, in Lower Egypt the daily prayers were said by the monks individually in their cells. Thus, although a communal assembly offered an element of mutual encouragement in the work of prayer, and afforded opportunity for supervision and discipline over the possible weakness and indolence of the more junior brethren, gathering together was ultimately a matter of indifference.

A second way in which the two traditions of praying differ is in their understandings of the ministers of worship. In "cathedral" prayer worship is led by the ordained ministers of the local church: it is presided over by the bishop, or in his absence a presbyter; the intercessions are announced by a deacon; and, although it is not obvious from Egeria's description, the verses of the psalms and canticles are also sung by formally appointed cantors. In "monastic" prayer, however, there are no permanently designated ministries, but each individual in the community has both the right and the obligation at assemblies for prayer to take an equal turn at chanting the verses of the psalms or reading the biblical lections to the others.

A third contrast between the two ways of praying is in the contents of the prayer. "Cathedral" prayer is composed chiefly of praise and intercession, the praise being expressed in a limited number of appropriate psalms and canticles, usually unchanging from day to day. Participants saw themselves as engaged the church's primary priestly vocation, participating in the prayer of Christ, the great high priest, and continually offering the sacrifice of praise and thanksgiving to God on behalf of all creation and interceding for the salvation of the world. It may rightly be described, therefore, as intrinsically outward looking in its orientation. It is prayer for others, not just for the benefit of the participants.

The heart of "monastic" prayer, on the other hand, is essentially silent meditation. The psalms and scripture readings that occur within the rite simply provide the "food," as it were, for that prayer: the real praying goes on in the spaces in between. The worshipper listens to the words of the psalm or biblical reading, engages in interior reflection on its meaning, and prays for the grace necessary to grow spiritually. "Monastic" prayer may therefore legitimately be described as pedagogical or formational in its intent. It is inward looking, directed toward the individual's sanctification. For that reason, it tends to involve a much larger number of psalms than the "cathedral" tradition, and other scripture readings too, since it tries to draw upon the richness of the biblical treasury to promote this ascetical progress. Indeed, it rapidly became common in early monasticism for a novice to be required to learn the whole psalter by heart, and for the daily services to be composed of a cycle of psalms in their biblical order which sought to complete all 150 of them within a set period of time.

"Cathedral" and "monastic" prayer also differ in their "outward" and "inward" orientation in another sense. The externals of worship are vitally important to "cathedral" prayer. It is not so much that cathedral prayer is expressed or somehow clothed in the externals but that the externals are themselves an intrinsic part of the prayer. Note, for example, the attention Egeria pays to the lights at the evening service. It was not merely that the Church of the Resurrection was particularly dark and thus required plenty of illumination so that people could see what they were doing. Rather, as we know from other sources, the ritual lighting of the lamps was an important part of evening worship in many parts of the fourth-century church. Thus words and actions went together in the "cathedral" tradition.

For "monastic" prayer, on the other hand, the externals are ultimately dispensable. The opposite may appear to be the case from Cassian's account, since considerable attention seems to have been directed toward the various postures (standing, kneeling, sitting) to be adopted at different points in the service. But this is misleading. It should be noted that while this common posture is insisted upon, there is no other sign of ceremonial in the service. There is, for example, no ritual lighting of the lamp at the evening office. The changing posture is certainly valued here as an aid to prayer, and the insistence upon concerted action helps to discipline the novice in prayer. But these things are not the prayer itself: "real" prayer in this tradition is interior, what goes on inside the heart and mind of the worshipper, to which the exterior action may be an aid or support, but one which can eventually be left behind. Once the morning office is over, the same prayer can be continued while sitting plaiting ropes or performing other manual tasks in the Egyptian monastic communities, whereas "cathedral" prayer cannot.

Finally, one other difference may be mentioned. Both traditions believed firmly in the apostolic injunction, "pray without ceasing" (1

Thess. 5:17). The "monastic" tradition, however, tends to interpret this literally and thus seeks to spend as much time as possible in actual prayer: the Egyptian desert monks, for example, strove to spend all of their waking hours in prayer, and kept the period of sleep to a minimum, and later monastic orders multiplied the number of offices to be said each day so as to increase the time allocated to prayer. The "cathedral" tradition of prayer, on the other hand, was content with only occasional assemblies for prayer, usually just twice a day, morning and evening, though sometimes more frequently. Yet this was not to abandon the scriptural precept of ceaseless prayer. For this command was understood to mean not that a Christian should spend as much time as humanly possible in actual praying but that the whole of life should be turned, as it were, into a prayer: "whether you eat or drink, or whatever you do, do everything for the glory of God" (1 Cor. 10:31).

FORM AND FUNCTION

As I have already suggested, these two contrasting ways of praying are not just something that belonged to fourth-century Christianity. On the contrary, they have both been characteristic of Christian prayer throughout its history. For they should not be understood as limited to the particular forms in which they are found in the early church. Indeed, as we shall see from examples in the next chapter, external appearances are often not a reliable guide in later Christian history: a form of prayer may look "monastic," but be understood by those praying it as fulfilling a "cathedral" function; conversely, something that has the external characteristics of a "cathedral" pattern of prayer may be used for a "monastic" purpose.

Thus, whatever their external appearances, different acts of worship tend to fulfill one of these two functions more than the other. Thus, for example, some are clearly communal actions; in other cases, while a large number of people may have gathered together in the same physical location, what is going on is really individual worship. Similarly, people praying alone may well be engaging in "monastic" prayer, but it is instead quite possible for them to understand what they are doing as part of a "cathedral" pattern of praying: although separated physically from others, they believe themselves to be joined in spirit to the worship of the whole church.

While the principal Sunday service of many churches in various Christian traditions has usually been "cathedral" in character, in other cases it has leant more in the direction of "monastic" worship, with the emphasis falling on the reading and preaching of scripture and inner reflection on it by the members of the congregation. And even those Christian traditions where the Sunday liturgy is of a "cathedral" kind often include in their regular weekly cycle other acts of worship that more closely mirror the "monastic" pattern, where nothing is done together that could not equally well be done by each person alone.

Some would want to describe the difference between the two ways of praying as a contrast between "liturgical" and "nonliturgical" worship. However, since the word *liturgical* is very hard to define, and is used by different people in different senses, this description can be misleading. Such mistakes are multiplied when church leaders create a polarity between "liturgical" and "contemporary" worship. Throughout this book, therefore, the terms "cathedral" and "monastic" will generally be preferred, and will always be placed inside quotation marks when they are being used with this particular meaning, in order to distinguish them from the use of the same words in other senses.

Moreover, sometimes different groups of people experience the same event in different ways. At a medieval high mass, for instance, the clergy and other ministers in the sanctuary no doubt saw themselves as constituting the church at prayer, engaged in the corporate celebration of its official liturgy; the lay men and women in the congregation, on the other hand, would have experienced the event quite differently, as they got on with their private devotions, pausing only to focus on what was going on in the sanctuary at the solemn moments when bells were rung to attract their attention.

Frequently, of course, a particular act of worship is neither purely of one type or of the other but composed of elements from both categories, and so is a combination of the two ways of praying. And this is not necessarily a bad thing, for both are essential parts of a balanced diet of prayer for Christians. To neglect one or the other is to risk a serious deficiency in one's prayer life, even though different human beings may be drawn more naturally to one than the other. Those who find individual contemplation, participation in a charismatic prayer group, or a devotional activities like the saying of the Rosary or the

Stations of the Cross most appealing to their spiritual temper also need to take part in the more formal, corporate worship of the church, offering praise and intercession for others, if they are to share in the fullness of Christianity; conversely, those whose spiritual diet is exclusively composed of liturgical worship also need to find time to explore quiet meditation and reflection if they are to grow into the mind of Christ.

A happy balance, however, is not always what people encounter. Sadly, the Christian tradition in the West, both Catholic and Protestant, has tended to value one way of prayer more than the other. The meditative road of "monastic" prayer has been seen as the way for the really "spiritual" individual, and liturgical worship regarded as much inferior to it. Participation in liturgy, it has been thought, is a Christian obligation which of course cannot be neglected, but it is private prayer that is truly beneficial. We shall trace this story in more detail in the next chapter. Nevertheless, to acquiesce in the perpetuation of this situation is to ignore the fact that private prayer tends to be inward looking, individualistic, and to lack an ecclesial dimension. Valuable though it certainly is in itself, it needs to be supplemented by the experience of liturgical worship for a healthy Christian spirituality. Besides the problem of balance, there is also a second difficulty that often prevents the two ways of prayer from enjoying a peaceful coexistence, and that is a common failure to recognize the difference between them, and therefore to apply the wrong criteria to them. For example, we may attend an act of worship and complain afterwards that there was insufficient opportunity for silent reflection, too much active participation, too much noise from children, and so on. In so doing, we are applying the criteria appropriate to "monastic" prayer to a service that may have been intended as "cathedral" worship. Conversely, clergy may be baffled when a large number of their congregation seem to prefer to attend the quiet 8 A.M. celebration of the Eucharist on a Sunday morning instead of the more lively 10 A.M. service, with greater active participation, hymns, and a fellowship hour afterwards. They may even try to introduce some of these things into the early service, thinking that the congregation is missing out on what constitutes real eucharistic worship, and encounter inexplicable opposition to such things as the mutual exchange of a liturgical handshake. They are assuming that what is going on—or should be going on—is "cathedral" worship, whereas the members of the congregation may well be searching instead for an experience of "monastic" prayer that the newly introduced liturgical changes are denying them.

Like the notion of the four food groups in dietary planning, therefore, the scholarly distinction between the two types of worship can be an important practical aid in helping us ensure a balanced and healthy spirituality. Both have something vital to contribute to our understanding of prayer and to our Christian living. For it is just as unhealthy to become completely absorbed in the cultivation and sanctification of one's own soul to the exclusion of the world around as it is to become so absorbed in the externals of liturgical practice that one loses hold on the inner spirit which feeds and vitalizes that prayer.

SUGGESTIONS FOR FURTHER READING

Bradshaw, Paul F. "Cathedral and Monastery: Two Ways of Praying," in E. Rozanne Elder, ed. *The Contemplative Path: Reflections on Recovering a Neglected Tradition*. Kalamazoo, Mich.: Cistercian Publications, 1996. Pp. 25-37.

_____. "Cathedral vs. Monastery: The Only Alternatives for the Liturgy of the Hours?" in J. Neil Alexander, ed. *Time and Community: Studies in Liturgical History and Theology*. Washington DC: Pastoral Press, 1990. Pp. 123-136.

_____. "Cathedral and Monastic: What's in a Name?," *Worship* 77 (2003): 341-353.

Veilleux, Armand. "Prayer in the Pachomian Koinonia," in William Skudlarek, ed. *The Continuing Quest for God*. Collegeville, Minn.: Liturgical Press, 1982. Pp. 61-66.

Wilkinson, John. *Egeria's Travels*. London: SPCK, 1971; revised ed. Jerusalem: Ariel, 1981.

Woolfenden, Gregory. *Daily Liturgical Prayer: Origins and Theology*. Aldershot/Burlington, Vermont: Ashgate, 2004.

2

The Divorce Between Liturgy and Spirituality

How did liturgy and spirituality become separated? The answer might seem obvious—through the emergence of "monastic" prayer in the fourth century—but the story is not quite so simple. First of all, the roots of "monastic" prayer can be traced even further back, and are ultimately grounded in Paul's injunction to "pray without ceasing" (1 Thessalonians 5:17). As we have seen, most early Christians understood this to mean transforming one's whole life into an act of worship, in which every word and action became, as it were, a prayer, a sacrificial offering to God (see Romans 12:1; 1 Corinthians 10:31; Hebrews 13:16), but with this being focused in explicit acts of prayer at fixed hours several times each day.

At least from the end of the second century, however, if not sooner, there were some who were not satisfied with this understanding but wished to fulfill Paul's injunction more literally. This attitude seems to have been particularly prevalent in Alexandria among those Christians who had come under the influence of the philosophy of Plato and the Stoics, and it was extensively developed by Clement of Alexandria. Although he admitted the necessity of set times of prayer for those not very far advanced in the spiritual life, yet for those who would be perfect Christians (or "Gnostics" as he calls them), prayer was to be a state of continual communion with God:

During his whole life the Gnostic in every place, even if he happens to be alone by himself, and wherever he has any of those who share the same faith, honours God, that is, acknowledges his gratitude for the knowledge of the way to live. ... Holding festival, then, in our whole life, and persuaded that God is altogether on every side present, we cultivate our fields, praising; we sail the sea, hymning. ...

Now if some assign fixed hours for prayer—as, for example, the third and sixth and ninth—yet the Gnostic prays throughout his whole life, endeavouring by prayer to have fellowship with God. And briefly, having arrived there, he leaves behind him all that is of no service, as having now received the perfection of one who acts by love. (*Strom.* 7.7; English translation from William Wilson, *The Writings of Clement of Alexandria*, vol. 2 [Edinburgh: T&T Clark, 1872], pp. 431, 432, 435)

This approach to prayer was appropriated by the Egyptian desert fathers of the fourth century, whose aim was to maintain as near as possible a ceaseless vigil of prayer, punctuated only by the minimal interruption for food and sleep. Thus "monastic" prayer is not only interior and contemplative in character, but also quite unrelated to specific times and seasons: all that is ultimately required is that one should pray as much as possible.

Strangely enough, however, although later monastic communities in the West inherited from the Egyptian desert tradition the distinctive *form* of their daily common worship—the alternation of psalms and silent prayer—they did not preserve for long the "monastic" *concept* of prayer that had originally given rise to it. Instead they began to interpret what they were doing in more "cathedral" terms, encouraged to some extent no doubt by the fact that some monastic communities became responsible leading the daily worship of churches and cathedrals. Thus they saw the psalms, not as the food for their contemplation in the silence that followed, but as their hymns of praise to God, regardless of whether the contents of the texts they were chanting were expressing divine praise or calling down fire upon the psalmist's enemies! They understood themselves to be singing the psalms because God liked to hear them, and not for their own spiritual advancement. We can see this transformation of function taking place in the monastic rule known as the *Rule of the Master* (which is probably a forerunner of the *Rule of Benedict*), written in the late fifth or early sixth century:

> So great must be the reverential seriousness and the manner of chanting the psalms that the Lord listens more lovingly than we say them; as Scripture declares: "You take delight in the coming of the morning, and in the evening," and again: "Sing the psalms to him joyfully and skillfully, for direct is the word of the Lord," and again: "Exult in him with fear," and again, "Sing to the Lord wisely." Therefore if it commands the singing of psalms to be done wisely and with fear, the person singing them should stand with body motionless and head bowed, and should sing praises to the Lord with composure, since he is indeed performing his service before the Godhead, as the prophet teaches when he says: "In the presence of the angels I will sing your praise" (chap. 47).

The *Rule of The Master* also insisted that the periods of silent prayer between the psalms should always be kept short, to avoid the risk of any of the brethren falling asleep or being tempted to evil thoughts (chap. 48); and the *Rule of Benedict* echoed all this advice more succinctly, although giving as the reason for brevity in prayer that "we are not to imagine that our prayers will be heard because we use many words" (chaps. 19-20). In the light of this changed understanding of the character of monastic daily prayer, it was almost inevitable that in the course of time the silence between the psalms would completely disappear, and the psalms came to follow directly one after the other. Thus we could say that even the spirituality of monastic communities in the early Middle Ages was primarily "cathedral" rather than "monastic," in spite of the fact that the outward form of their daily worship might suggest otherwise.

The words chosen in Western Christianity to describe these daily liturgies reflect that understanding. While in early monasticism the phrase *opus Dei*, "the work of God," had referred to the whole of the ascetic life, in the *Rule of the Master*, the *Rule of Benedict*, and later usage, it is restricted to the cycle of worship alone, thus marking this activity off from the reading, prayer, and manual labor of the rest of the day. Similarly, the *opus Dei* was also called the *officium* or "duty," and the particular allocation of psalms at each service was known as the *pensum*, which originally meant something that was weighed out, but could also be understood as a task or as an obligation that was owed to someone. Because of the strongly penitential character of much monastic spirituality, the daily office thus came to be seen as a duty owed to God as a result of human sinfulness, a debt that had to be paid in the currency God had chosen—psalms, measured out in small installments numerous times each day throughout one's life. Because the length and number of offices each day greatly multiplied in the course of the Middle Ages, this psalmody also eventually became a *pensum* in another sense—a burden almost too heavy to bear.

In the course of time the absence of the intercessory element of "cathedral" worship from these "monastic" forms in the West came to be felt as a deficiency. This was especially the case in monasteries that had been built by endowments from wealthy landowners, where the community felt obliged to pray for the spiritual welfare of their founders and benefactors. However, instead of restoring extensive petitions for human needs to the offices themselves, perhaps in the form of a litany, the monastic tradition generally chose to create supplementary little offices of psalmody attached to the main office of the day, and these were recited with intercessory intent, even though they were not intercessory in form. The earliest sign of this is in the revision of the *Rule of Benedict* that was undertaken by Benedict of Aniane (c. 750-821), where before the first office of the day the monks were required to recite in silence five psalms for the living, five for the dead, and five for those recently deceased, each group of psalms being concluded with a prayer. This practice eventually gave rise to a formal Office for the Dead joined to the night, morning, and evening offices of each day. Thus, once again, we have a situation where the form of the prayer is divorced from the function that it has.

The prayer life of clergy and lay people was not essentially different from that of the religious orders. The clergy were increasingly pressured into adopting the "monastic" patterns of daily worship practiced by religious communities, but of course with the same "cathedral" interpretation of the activity that those communities had appropriated; and however remarkable it may seem to our present-day eyes, for several centuries large numbers of lay people apparently also persisted in gathering with their clergy at least for the morning and evening offices every day. Thus, Caesarius of Arles in the sixth century may have complained that people were gossiping among themselves when they came to church, failing to learn and join in the psalms, and refusing to get up earlier to attend the monastic night office that preceded their morning worship, but the fact is that the people were actually present at the daily services (see, e.g., *Serm.* 6.3; 72.1; 76.3). Indeed, this custom of corporate daily prayer has survived in some Eastern churches more or less down to the present day, although it did eventually decline in the West, and most people came to church only on Sundays and major feast days.

Even so, in the late Middle Ages many pious individuals continued to try to associate themselves with the worship of the church in their individual daily observances. Unable to perform the full monastic round in its entirety because of lack of time and the difficulty and expense involved in obtaining hand-copied texts of all the material, the wealthier and educated members of the church procured for themselves small "Books of Hours," as they were known, containing some selected psalms and the "little hours," that is, the Office for the Dead and some of the other supplementary offices that had by now become attached to the main offices of the day in monastic communities and focused on a particular object of devotion, as for example the offices of the Blessed Virgin Mary, of Christ's Passion, of the Holy Cross, and of the Blessed Sacrament.

Ordinary people who were not wealthy enough to be able to afford such texts and not educated enough to be able to read them anyway, but wanted to participate in this same worship, found others ways of doing so. Some were able to memorize whole psalms and recite them; others who could not manage to do this were instead encouraged to learn an individual psalm verse and repeat it over and over again as the equivalent of a saying a psalm; and if even that were beyond their capabilities, they were simply to recite the Lord's Prayer (which had formed the concluding psalm prayer in some monastic traditions) a specific number of times in place of the psalms themselves.

Such frequent repetition of the Lord's Prayer necessitated some means of keeping tally of the total number of times it had been said, and so there emerged a counting device, which consisted of a number of beads threaded on to a piece of string, with knots in the string marking each tenth bead. The manufacture of such devices, themselves known as *Paternosters*, was a lucrative medieval industry, and the street still known as Paternoster Row in London, England, marks the site of the merchants who once sold them in that city. During the twelfth century devotion to the Virgin Mary gave rise to what was called the Marian Psalter, with each of the 150 psalms being supplied with an accompanying text in praise of the Virgin, and by the thirteenth century the recitation of the *Paternosters* too had become linked to this Marian devotion, the *Ave Maria* being joined to the Lord's Prayer. So began the development of the Rosary.

Like the prayer of the better educated, therefore, that of devout poor people also had its roots in "cathedral" worship, even if the connection was not very visible, and it still had some association with the prayer of the church, in that people would pause to offer a brief prayer whenever the church bell rang to announce the regular hours of the daily offices. This practice also eventually became associated with Marian devotion, and so gave rise to the *Angelus*, an act of prayer to the Virgin performed at fixed hours of the day and based on the angelic salutation to Mary in Luke 1:26 38.

LECTIO DIVINA AND DEVOTIO MODERNA

Nevertheless, the loss of the truly "monastic" dimension from the daily offices themselves, of an activity understood primarily as a source of spiritual benefit for the participants, did not mean that it disappeared from Christian life altogether. It was preserved in Western monasticism in the practice of *lectio divina*, literally "divine reading," a period of several hours set apart each day in the monastic rule for the individual reading and learning by heart of scriptural texts (and later of other early Christian writings), which were then meditated upon both at that time and also during the manual work occupying the rest of the day. Mealtimes were similarly accompanied by reading in common from the Bible or early Christian literature. As with the office itself, *lectio divina* was also urged upon the clergy and lay people, though once again only a very small number of the latter can have been in a position to put it into practice. Thus the two forms of praying, the "cathedral" and the "monastic," continued to exist alongside one another in this way for several centuries, with neither being given precedence over the other, although the "monastic" was in practice restricted to a relatively small segment of Christians.

In the later Middle Ages, however, we can detect the beginnings of a trend to elevate individual, contemplative, and interior prayer as spiritually superior to the communal, external forms of the divine office, which it was thought could present a distraction to "real" praying. This movement, to which was given the name *devotio moderna*, "modern devotion," arose at the end of the fourteenth century, and was encouraged by the emerging Renaissance emphasis upon the importance of the individual. The most famous writer of this school was Thomas à Kempis, whose *Imitation of Christ* has continued to be regarded as a spiritual classic down to the present day. It is really here that the divorce between liturgy and spirituality can be said to begin in earnest.

Perhaps the most notable public effect of the *devotio moderna* was upon the practice of the Society of Jesus (Jesuits), founded by Ignatius Loyola in 1541, which was the first formal religious order not to require its members to assemble together "in choir" for the celebration of the canonical hours of the divine office. Jesuits were still obliged to say all the offices individually, and their dispensation from the communal celebration was only intended to give them more freedom to engage in the apostolic labors for which they had been founded. Yet given the power of their example, it could not but encourage the view that the office was merely a duty to be performed as quickly and painlessly as possible and that the heart of spirituality lay in the sort of interior prayer and meditation embodied the *Spiritual Exercises* of the Jesuits' founder. Not unnaturally, therefore, in later centuries clergy and members of religious orders, except those whose rule still obliged them to celebrate the office in common, tended toward its private recitation.

However much from a modern perspective one might regret the split that then began to open up between liturgy and spirituality, the development was more or less inevitable in the historical circumstances in which the *devotio moderna* was born. By the late Middle Ages both Eucharist and office had generally come to be performed in a purely external, mechanistic fashion. Moreover, the office had expanded in length and frequency to such a point that it took up a great deal of time in the day and hence constituted an almost intolerable burden for those obliged to take part in it. Thus it is hardly surprising that people were hungry for something more spiritually uplifting with which to nourish their piety, and so tended to undervalue liturgy as prayer.

It is important to note, however, that at this point in history the disassociation of liturgy and spirituality in this way really only affected a relatively small number of people within the church, an elite who were wealthy and better educated, and among them at least the clergy and members of religious orders were still obliged to persevere in the saying of the office, even if they found it spiritually dead for them, alongside the new fashion for interior prayer. The two may have become separated, but they continued to coexist. Moreover, many lay people followed the example of the clergy and religious orders and retained both customs: the continuing appearance of new forms of Books of Hours is sufficient testimony to that. Toward the end of the Middle Ages vernacular versions had begun to emerge; these were often known as primers and set the pattern for the books of daily prayer used by lay people in later centuries. The sixteenth century witnessed a veritable explosion of such publications, especially in England. One such book, called simply *A Manual of Prayers* ran to well over a hundred editions between 1583 and the mid-nineteenth century, and similar books can be found all over Europe. While the greatly expanded supply of these can be explained by the invention of printing, the demand for them is a different matter, and is probably to be accounted for in part by some expansion of literacy at this period, but more by an increase in a sense of individual responsibility for the conduct of the spiritual life among pious lay people.

The Churches of the Reformation

Martin Luther had in his earlier life experienced firsthand the painful burden of the obligation to recite the full round of medieval daily offices:

> When I was a monk I was unwilling to omit any of the prayers, but when I was busy with public lecturing and writing I often accumulated my appointed prayers for a whole week, or even two or three weeks. Then I would take a Saturday off, or shut myself in for as long as three days without food and drink, until I had said the prescribed prayers. This made my head split, and as a consequence I couldn't close my eyes for five nights, lay sick unto death, and went out of my senses. (*Table Talk*, 495; English translation from Theodore G. Tappert, ed., *Luther's Works* 54 [Philadelphia: Fortress Press, 1967], p. 85.)

He eventually fell three months behind and gave up altogether.

Since, for both Luther and the other Reformers, the requirement to pray the offices was seen a "work" intended to satisfy God, and hence stood in opposition to their central tenet of justification by faith alone, it is not surprising that a clerical obligation to recite daily hours of prayer disappeared from all the churches of the Reformation, except the Church of England. Yet, even in this last case, there was a transformation in the purpose that the office was understood to fulfill. The Preface to the 1549 *Book of Common Prayer* declared that the original purpose of the daily office, as revealed by "the ancient fathers," had been for:

> a great advancement of godliness: For they so ordered the matter that all the whole Bible (or the greatest part thereof) should be read over once in the year, intending thereby that the Clergy . . . should (by often reading, and meditation in God's word) be stirred up to godliness themselves, and be the more able to exhort others by wholesome doctrine, and to confute them that were adversaries to the truth; and further, that the people (by daily hearing of holy scripture read in the Church) might continually profit more and more in the knowledge of God, and be the more inflamed with the love of his true religion.

In other words, what was being restored here was a pure "monastic" form and concept of the office, centered around the systematic reading of the Bible and recitation of the psalter. Later generations of Anglicans, however, like the monastic communities before them, have often tended to interpret what they were doing in more "cathedral" terms, as the offering of praise and prayer to God, even if the forms that they were required to use did not really correspond very well with that understanding.

But the Reformation had a much greater impact upon liturgical spirituality than merely the challenge to the clerical obligation to the daily office. Given the primacy accorded to the Word in Reformation theology, it was inevitable that all acts of public worship would tend to center around the proclamation and expounding of scripture, and that the congregation would be expected to ruminate and reflect upon what was said to them. Thus, a "monastic" style of worship was once more introduced into church services, and from there spread to the daily prayer life of Christians in Reformation traditions, since not unnaturally that too was often modeled on the pattern of the public worship. In 1647, for example, the General Assembly of the Church of Scotland put forward a *Directory for Family Worship*, which prescribed for daily practice the principal elements of the Sunday service, substituting for the sermon a "conference" between the participants. The Catholic *devotio moderna*, too, was not without its influence upon Protestant spirituality, as the growth of what is known as Pietism clearly testifies. Yet, since practices such as these required access to the Bible and other printed material, the high cost of books and continuing low levels of literacy meant that, as in the Catholic tradition, they remained restricted to a relatively small number of church members.

THE FINAL SEPARATION

Thus, in spite of the growth of a more "monastic" way of praying in both Catholic and Protestant traditions, the divorce between liturgy and spirituality was not truly finalized until at least the early nineteenth century. But why then? It was really a combination of many factors. For example, the industrial revolution brought large numbers of people from country to city and so put an end to the rural rhythm of the day, which had previously enabled people to associate themselves with the liturgical prayer being offered in nearby churches or monasteries. The concurrent growth of individualism privatized and voluntarized the practice of religion and hence of praying. There were also the effects of the romantic revival and the resurgence of evangelistic fervor, which led to a desire to inculcate the same holiness of life among ordinary people as was pursued by the more educated. Furthermore, new advances in printing technology played their part, enabling for the first time the mass production of books at a price that most people could afford. Coupled with the enormous growth in literacy that was brought about by the emergence of increasing opportunities for formal education in the nineteenth century, this made the relevant spiritual reading and prayer material necessary to support such devotions much more widely accessible.

Despite all the efforts of the liturgical movement in the twentieth century, a reconciliation of the two has not so far been effected. On the contrary, the effects of the divorce remain down to the present day, and affect all our attitudes toward prayer. Yet, even though such a rift may perhaps have been inevitable, given the historical circumstances of Western Christianity, it is not necessarily an irreversible process, and we should note that such a separation of liturgy and spirituality is not characteristic of the East in the same way that it is of the West.

Suggestions for Further Reading

Bradshaw, Paul F. "Whatever happened to daily prayer?," *Worship* 64 (1990): 10-23.

Fassler, Margot, & R. A. Baltzer, eds. *The Divine Office in the Latin Middle Ages*. Oxford: Oxford University Press, 2000.

Guiver, George. *Company of Voices: Daily Prayer and the People of God*. London: SPCK/New York: Pueblo, 1988. 2d ed., Norwich: Canterbury Press, 2001.

Jungmann, Joseph A. *Christian Prayer through the Centuries*. New York: Paulist Press, 1978. New edition, with notes, 2007.

The Rule of the Master. Translated by Luke Eberle. Kalamazoo, Mich.: Cistercian Publications, 1977.

Senn, Frank C., ed. *Protestant Spiritual Traditions*. New York: Paulist Press, 1986.

Van Engen, John. *Devotio Moderna: Basic Writings*. New York: Paulist Press, 1988.

Vogüé, Adalbert de. *The Rule of St Benedict: A Doctrinal and Spiritual Commentary*. Kalamazoo, Mich.: Cistercian Publications, 1983. Pp. 127-72, 239-57.

3

THE BIBLICAL ROOTS OF LITURGICAL PRAYER

When we look at some of the major forms of public prayer used in the Christian tradition, as for example eucharistic prayers or ordination prayers, we see that they tend to have two distinct parts: first, praise of God; and second, petition for God to act. This arrangement should probably not surprise us, since many prayers from different religious traditions are structured in this very same way. We might tend to conclude that the truly important part of the prayer, what it is really all about, is the second—the request for God to act—and that the first part, the praise, is simply a preliminary to that. For example, is not the central purpose of a eucharistic prayer to ask God to do something, whether it is changing the bread and wine into the body and blood of Christ or making us into worthy communicants? We might even be tempted to suspect that, at least in some ancient pagan religions, the presence of the praise in the first part of the prayer was really only an attempt to appeal to the vanity of the gods by flattery, and so persuade them to fulfill the suppliant's desires. That would be rather like our saying:

> "O God, I know that you are always more generous than any other god to those who ask you for anything: please help me to become rich."

However, when we examine the roots of the Judeo-Christian tradition of prayer in the Old Testament and its continuation in the New, we learn that the element of praise has a quite different purpose from simply being a "warm up" to the rest of the prayer or an attempt to curry favor with the divine, and that petition is not after all its central focus.

The Berakah

Let us take as the starting point for our examination two verses from the Pentateuch. The first is Genesis 24:26-27, which occurs within the story of the search by Abraham's servant for a wife for Isaac, Abraham's son. The servant had gone to the city of Nahor and was standing outside the city by the well at the evening hour, when it was customary for women to come and draw water. Along came Rebekah; a conversation ensued between the two of them, and the servant concluded that this was indeed the woman destined to be Isaac's bride. Verse 26 continues: "The man bowed his head and worshipped the LORD and said: 'Blessed be the LORD, the God of my master Abraham, who has not forsaken his steadfast love and his faithfulness toward my master.'"

The second passage is from the book of Exodus, 18:10-11, where Jethro, Moses' father in law, having heard of the successful escape by the people of Israel from their slavery in Egypt, says: "Blessed be the LORD, who has delivered you out of the hands of the Egyptians and out of the hand of Pharaoh. Now I know that the LORD is greater than all gods, because he delivered the people from under the hand of the Egyptians, when they dealt arrogantly with them." These are just two instances of a common pattern of prayer found in the Old Testament and in intertestamental literature—an initial blessing of God followed by a relative clause giving the grounds for the blessing—which eventually evolved into the standard form of prayer in later Judaism known as the *berakah* or "blessing." Such prayers need not always be as brief as the examples quoted, but could be expanded into a quite lengthy narrative of events for which God was being blessed. A good illustration of this is provided by 1 Kings 8:15-21, part of the prayer ascribed to Solomon at the dedication of the Jerusalem temple, which begins by blessing God for fulfilling the promise made to Solomon's father David, and then goes on to tell in more detail the story of that promise and to explain how it has been fulfilled through Solomon.

Unlike most prayers, these are not requests for something, nor do they offer praise to God in a way common in many religious traditions, including some later Christian practice, by heaping up laudatory epithets one upon another, as for example, "O God most mighty, most wonderful, most exalted, most gracious, most merciful," and so on. Instead, they are primarily acts of remembrance, or in Greek *anamnesis*. They recall what has happened, in the two cases quoted above in the immediate past, in others in more remote times. This remembrance fulfills several functions.

First, it involves *the religious interpretation of experience*. Abraham's servant does not say, as he might well have done, "What a smart man I am. I knew that if I stood by this well long enough, the right woman would eventually come along." Nor even: "What a stroke of luck. I arrive at the well, and who should come for water but my master's kinsman's daughter. What a remarkable coincidence!" Similarly, Jethro does not immediately praise Moses' skill in leading the people out of the clutches of their captors, nor again ascribe the outcome of their escape merely to good fortune. On the contrary, in both cases the ordinary human events that are recalled are interpreted and re-envisioned as being in reality the hidden activity of God. The prayer, then, is a means of retelling the story of normal experience in such a way as to give it a religious interpretation. In that sense, there is indeed not much difference between a prayer and a credal affirmation in the biblical tradition, and you will notice that the prayers quoted above are not actually addressed to God at all but are instead statements about God. Retelling the story of our experience in religious terms is really a creed, for it is a statement of our faith in God's activity and of our beliefs about God.

Second, while we may describe this remembrance as the religious interpretation of life, we may also describe it as *confession* or *acknowledgement*. When people interpret what has happened to them in this way, they shift the spotlight off themselves and onto God. They are forced to admit that it was not their skill, their ingenuity, or their greatness that was responsible for bringing about success, but instead the power of God in their lives. For example, when we bless God for the food that we eat, we are acknowledging that what we have is given to us by God, and that without God's action all our skills of farming and cooking would be ineffective. Thus, the prayer is an admission of what we believe to be true, and this whether we happen to like it or not, and whether the news is good or bad. For although the two examples quoted involved the success of a human venture, such prayer was also made when the experience was less happy, for instance, when people were forced to acknowledge that what had befallen them was God's way of teaching them a lesson.

Thirdly, we may also describe the remembrance as being a *proclamation*. People often wonder why Jewish and Christian prayers tend to keep describing at such great length what God has done. Surely God has not forgotten about it and needs reminding of it? As we have seen above, we do it first of all to remind ourselves: we are the ones who are in danger of forgetting, and need the constant repetition lest we lose sight of the hand of God in our lives. But it also has another purpose: when the prayer is said in the presence of others, it proclaims to the listeners the faith of the one who is recounting the story; it reveals to them God's action in the world; and it invites them to share that same faith vision, to interpret the experience in the same way, and so be led to acknowledge God as the author and giver of all. This is how biblical prayer gives praise to God, not by the piling up of laudatory words and phrases, but by the telling of God's story to others, so that they in turn may see it and believe it, that they too may give the glory to God by offering their "Amen" or "Alleluia" response to the words.

In this sense, just as we said that there was little difference in the biblical tradition between prayer and creed, so too there is little difference between prayer and the proclamation of God's word. When we pray our prayer of remembrance we are also preaching, and when we read aloud the biblical text or tell of God's work in the world, we are also engaged in a prayer of remembrance. Worship and mission are thus not separate things, between which a choice may have to be made. On the contrary, they are the very same activity. To do one is to do the other. To proclaim the gospel is to offer worship to God, and to recount God's mighty deeds in prayer is to preach the good news. Indeed, the practice of calling the first part of a eucharistic prayer the "preface" did not arise because it preceded what was thought to be the main body of the prayer, but because the Latin word *praefatio* meant proclamation: the preface proclaims the mighty works of God.

The fourth and final description of this pattern of prayer is as *consecration*. When in our prayer we remember, acknowledge, and proclaim that the day we have just begun is not ours to do with as we like, or that the bread that is set before us is really a gift from God and not merely the product of our own hands, then our remembrance also in a sense hallows or consecrates the events, the things, the people, and ourselves. By reminding the worshippers who is the true author and giver of all good things, the prayer restores the material elements of creation and the activities of human beings to their proper relationship to God. Through periodic acts of remembrance during each day, time itself can come to be redeemed and human lives made holy, to be spent in accordance with God's will.

This last insight also helps us to see more clearly the connection between the prayer of remembrance that we have been describing and other instances in the Old Testament that also include petition and intercession, as for example 1 Kings 8:56-61, another part of the prayer ascribed to Solomon at the dedication of the Jerusalem temple, which begins by saying, "Blessed be the LORD who has given rest to his people Israel, according to all that he promised; not one word has failed of all his good promise, which he spoke through his servant Moses." But it then goes on to make request: "The LORD our God be with us, as he was with our ancestors; may he not leave us or abandon us." As we have already seen, the praise is not simply an initial attempt to flatter God before moving on to the real purpose of the prayer—the request for what we want—but is itself at the heart of what the invocation is all about.

So then, any intercessions that are added to this nucleus are merely the explicit articulation of what is already implicit in the act of remembrance itself—the desire that God will continue the salvific activity that has been recalled, and thus sanctify those for whom prayer is made and draw all things back into a right relationship with God. Such intercession is thus essentially in subordination to the prayer of remembrance: it is the recalling of God's goodness in the past that constitutes the ground on which God may be asked to act now, and one may only properly petition God to do things that are in accord with the divine nature revealed in the act of remembrance. It would not be appropriate, for example, to pray:

> "Blessed be the Lord our God, who always shows mercy to those in need; and now, I pray, slay my enemies."

Often this point will be underscored by a concluding statement in the prayer that indicates that what is being requested is not just for the benefit of the suppliants but for the advancement of God's glory, in order that the whole world may see the divine works and be led to acknowledge and praise God, as the worshippers themselves do now. Thus Solomon's prayer ends (1 Kings 8:60), "that all the peoples of the earth may know that the LORD is God; there is no other." Hence, as the prayer began with praise, so it returns to praise in this final doxology.

THE HODAYAH

At this stage, those who pray may well be wondering about the connection between these Old Testament prayer patterns and those of the Christian tradition, which seem hardly to resemble them at all. All is not lost, however, for the Old Testament is also familiar with a variant prayer pattern often called the *hodayah*. Isaiah 12:1 will serve as an example of this. It is usually rendered in English translations as something like, "I will thank you, O LORD, because, though you were angry with me, your anger turned away and you comforted me."

At first this may look very different from the examples of prayers that we considered earlier, but a closer examination suggests otherwise. The Hebrew verb normally translated in English versions of the scriptures as "thank" is *hodah,* and this word strictly speaking means "to acknowledge" or "to confess"—it is, for example, the standard verb used when confessing or admitting that one has sinned. So a more literal translation of Isaiah 12:1, and of many other biblical prayers like it, would be, "I acknowledge to you, O Lord, that though you were angry with me, your anger turned away and you comforted me."

In other words, the form may be somewhat different from that of the *berakah,* but the intention is the same—the admission that God has acted in one life's and the remembrance and recounting in religous terms of what has happened. One form speaks about God and uses the verb *barak* in the passive:

"Blessed be God, who . . ."

The other addresses God directly and uses *hodah* in the active:

"I acknowledge to you, O Lord, that. . . ."

But they are simply two variant forms of the same kind of praying. Indeed, the form of the *berakah* later changed so that it addressed God directly:

> "Blessed are you, O Lord . . ."

This change probably came about because it was influenced by the construction of the *hodayah*. What is more, we can find longer prayers where both forms occur together. For example, the prayer in the book of Daniel, chapter 2, begins:

> "Blessed be the name of God from age to age,
>   for wisdom and power are his.
> He changes times and seasons,
>   deposes kings and sets up kings;
> he gives wisdom to the wise
>   and knowledge to those who have understanding.
> He reveals deep and hidden things;
>   he knows what is in the darkness,
>   and light dwells with him."

But then it continues:

> "To you, O God of my ancestors,
>   I give thanks [acknowledge] and praise,
> for you have given me wisdom and power,
>   and have now revealed to me what we asked of you,
>   for you have revealed to us what the king ordered."

The second book of Maccabees, chapter 1, has a prayer that puts the construction the other way around, beginning with thanksgiving and ending with the blessing form. Or, as another example, there is what eventually became the standard Jewish grace after meals, the *birkat ha mazon*, which begins: "Blessed are you, Lord our God, king of the universe, who nourishes us and the whole world with goodness, grace, kindness, and mercy"; and then continues, "We thank you, Lord our God, because you have given us for our inheritance a desirable land. . . ."

The New Testament

Thus we can see that there were two parallel prayer forms in ancient Israel, different in appearance but united in their basic purpose, which was to interpret, acknowledge, and proclaim all that happened as the hidden activity of God. In the first century of the Common Era both forms were still in use among both Jews and early Christians, and the New Testament contains a few instances of prayers cast in the *berakah* form, translated into Greek by use of the verb *eulogeo*. The Song of Zechariah in Luke 1:68-79, for example, begins, "Blessed be the Lord God of Israel . . ."; and in 1 Peter 1:3 we have: "Blessed be the God and Father of our Lord Jesus Christ! By his great mercy he has given us new birth into a living hope through the resurrection of Jesus Christ from the dead."

In general, however, Christians seem to have come to prefer the *hodayah* construction. Indeed, we find this very form in one of the few prayers that the New Testament records being said by Jesus himself, Matthew 11:25-26//Luke 10:21: "I thank you, Father, Lord of heaven and earth, because you have hidden these things from the wise and intelligent and have revealed them to infants; yes, Father, for such was your gracious will." The Greek verb used here is a compound form of *homologeo*, the standard word for "acknowledge" or "confess" and so naturally chosen by early Greek-speaking Jews to translate *hodah*. Later Jews and Christians, on the other hand, tended to employ instead the verb *eucharisteo*, "give thanks." Prayers of this type are found on the lips of Jesus in John 11:41 ("Father, I thank you because you have heard me . . ."), of the twenty four elders in Revelation 11:17-18 ("We give thanks to you, Lord God Almighty . . .") and even of a Pharisee at prayer in the Temple in Luke 18:11-12 ("God, I thank you that I am not like other people . . .").

Nearly all of Paul's letters begin with a similar thanksgiving for some gift bestowed by God on the recipients of the letter and proceed to a reference to the author's continuing intercession for them, almost certainly reflecting the structure of his actual prayers. References to blessings at meals also show a growing tendency to substitute *eucharisteo* for *eulogeo*, again no doubt reflecting the writers' own experience of prayers that were cast in the *hodayah* form rather than in the *berakah* form. So, for example, while Matthew and Mark use *eulogeo* with reference to the bread and *eucharisteo* with reference to the cup in their accounts of the Last Supper (Matt. 26:26-27; Mark 14:22-25), Luke and Paul employ *eucharisteo* for both bread and cup (Luke 22:17-19; 1 Cor. 11.24).

Although the preference for the *hodayah* form over the *berakah* and the trend toward using *eucharisteo* rather than some compound form of *homologeo* as its verb was a perfectly natural development, especially since the prayer form carried such strong overtones of thanksgiving, it ultimately led to a serious impoverishment in the understanding of the nature of the dominant Christian pattern of praying. Not only did it disguise the close connection that exists between Jewish and Christian concepts of prayer, but most Christians today would think of a eucharistic style of praying as being nothing more than an expression of gratitude, a way saying "thank you" to God for the good things that they have received. But this, of course, is only a small part of its biblical meaning and purpose, and leads to difficulties for worshippers. If prayers like this are thought of as being merely expressions of appreciation for the reception of God's grace, what are Christians to do when they don't feel particularly grateful inside themselves, when God doesn't seem to have been especially kind to them? Should they stop praying?

A recovery of the richness of the biblical heritage of our prayer tradition, therefore, can rescue us from such a subjective and potentially egocentric perception and enable us to see that much more than expressing gratitude is involved in a eucharistic pattern of prayer. Recalling to mind what God has done, we are interpreting our human experience in religious terms; we are making our credal confession of faith; we are proclaiming our gospel to the world; we are restoring ourselves and all creation to a relationship of holiness to God; and all this not for ourselves but so that God may be glorified.

SUGGESTIONS FOR FURTHER READING

Balentine, Samuel. *Prayer in the Hebrew Bible*. Minneapolis: Fortress Press, 1993.

Bradshaw, Paul F. *Daily Prayer in the Early Church*. London: SPCK, 1981/New York: Oxford University Press, 1982. Chaps. 1 and 2.

Clements, Ronald E. *In Spirit and in Truth: Insights from Biblical Prayers*. Atlanta: John Knox Press, 1985.

Harrington, Wilfrid. *The Bible's Ways of Prayer*. Wilmington, Del.: Michael Glazier, 1980.

4

The Prayer of Christ in the Church

Christians are not merely disciples or followers of Jesus, but according to Pauline theology, they are "in Christ." Through their baptism they participate in the death and resurrection of Christ and so are incorporated into him, not merely as individuals but as members of his body, the church. Hence, if it is to give true expression to this mystical reality, Christian prayer must also essentially be participation in the prayer of Christ himself and in the prayer of the whole church. In other words, it must have both a *christological* and an *ecclesiological* dimension.

The Christological Dimension

When Christians pray, they usually make their prayers "through Jesus Christ our Lord." Although this phrase often functions merely as a cue to the congregation that they are then supposed to say "Amen," its real meaning is much more profound. Indeed, in early centuries those words did not actually constitute the conclusion of prayers at all. Although the Western medieval liturgical books generally end the texts of prayers with *per Jesum Christum Dominum nostrum*, "through Jesus Christ our Lord," or more briefly still with *per dominum* or *per Christum* or some such form, or even with the word *per* alone, at first those expressions were understood as being just a shorthand expression for

33

a longer formula that one was to say: "who lives and reigns with you in the unity of the Holy Spirit for ever and ever." It continues to be the custom in Eastern liturgies to end prayers with an extensive trinitarian doxology, but later in the West, with the increase of the number of prayers within the rites, only the most important ones (for instance, the eucharistic prayer itself) retained the full conclusion, and the others were given just the shorter form, "through Jesus Christ our Lord."

For the first Christians, it was this reference to Jesus in their prayers that distinguished them from the prayers of other Jews. As we have seen in the preceding chapter, Jewish and Christian prayer forms were basically identical in the first century, and so all that marked out Christian prayers was the association of Christ with God, to whom they were directed. Although some early Christians did begin to address prayers individually to Christ or even to the Holy Spirit, this practice was gradually suppressed in more orthodox circles; and only very much later did it begin to reemerge there again. It was not really a desirable development, for it can easily convey to worshippers a vision of the existence of three gods rather than the classical trinitarian concept, and Christians who want to remain faithful to the New Testament understanding of Christ's relationship to the Father would do well to avoid it: nowhere do the scriptures make an unqualified identification between the persons of the Trinity.

The introduction of a reference to Jesus within traditional Jewish prayer patterns was done in one of several ways. In the *berakah* form, Christ could be associated with God in the opening address: instead of merely saying "Blessed be God, who . . .", a Christian might substitute,

> "Blessed be the God and Father of our Lord Jesus Christ, who
> . . ." (see 2 Corinthians 1:3; Ephesians 1:3; 1 Peter 1:3).

In the more widely used *hodayah* or *eucharistia* form, the opening address could be modified in a similar way, as for example Colossians 1:3:

> "We always thank God, the Father of our Lord Jesus Christ . . .,"

or alternatively the praise of God might be offered through Jesus Christ:

> "We give thanks to you, O God, through Jesus Christ our
> Lord. . . ."

Some such prayer form as this seems to lie behind Romans 1:8 and is widespread in post New Testament writings. It occurs, for example, at the beginning of both the eucharistic prayer and the prayer at lamplighting in the ancient church order known as the *Apostolic Tradition* of Hippolytus.

Early Christian prayers, like their Jewish counterparts, also tended to conclude with the note of praise, and here, too, Christ was included, usually along with a reference to the Holy Spirit and sometimes a mention of the church as well, as in the eucharistic prayer of the *Apostolic Tradition*:

> "that we may praise and glorify you through your child Jesus
> Christ, through whom be glory and honor to you, with the Holy
> Spirit, in your holy Church, both now and to the ages of ages."

Thus, at both the beginning and the end of prayers Christ was regularly portrayed as the mediator through whom the praise of God was offered. In prayers from the fourth century onward, however, a further development can be seen, in which the conclusion, "through Jesus Christ our Lord . . .," began to follow directly on the petitionary element in the second half of the prayer, without the intervention of some clause expressing praise. It is not entirely clear whether this came about simply by accident or whether it was done with deliberate intent. Its effect, however, was to represent Christ not just as the mediator of the church's praise but also as the mediator of the church's petitions and intercessions.

The Christian liturgical tradition derived this understanding of Christ's mediatory role from the image of him as the great high priest of the new and eternal covenant, portrayed especially clearly in the Letter to the Hebrews, chapters 8 and 9. Indeed, very early Christian prayers sometimes refer explicitly to Christ's priesthood in their conclusions, as for example the prayer in the First Letter of Clement, thought to have been written from Rome around A.D. 96:

> "We give thanks to you through Jesus Christ, the high priest
> and guardian of our souls, through whom . . ." (61.3).

Interestingly, the verb translated as "give thanks" here is the more traditional *exomologeo* rather than the later *eucharisteo*.

Absolutely fundamental to the notion of priesthood in any religion is the offering of sacrifice. This oblation can take the form of a gift expressing praise and thanksgiving for what the god has already done or be an act of intercession in order to obtain forgiveness for offenses committed or preserve a right relationship with the god. In the case of Christ, of course, the sacrifice that he offered is usually viewed as the oblation of his whole life, once for all. While the Letter to the Hebrews is emphatic about this, yet it also speaks of Christ continuing his priestly activity in his risen and glorified state, "since he ever lives to make intercession" (Heb. 7:25). It is interesting to observe that, while Eastern prayers continue to maintain an element of praise in their prayer endings, Western prayers instead pick up this phrase from Hebrews in their standard conclusion quoted earlier in this chapter:

> "Through Jesus Christ our Lord, who lives and reigns with you
> in the unity of the Holy Spirit for ever and ever."

THE ECCLESIOLOGICAL DIMENSION

Though in one sense Christ's priesthood is unique to him, since he has done what no other human being was able to do, yet in another sense his followers, too, can be said to share in that priesthood through their membership of his body. So it is that 1 Peter 2:5 calls Christians to be "a holy priesthood, to offer spiritual sacrifices acceptable to God through Jesus Christ." While these spiritual sacrifices are not limited to acts of worship as such but naturally encompass the whole of the Christian life, so that Romans 12:1 appeals to the readers to "present your bodies as a living sacrifice, holy and acceptable to God, which is your spiritual worship," nevertheless the sacrificial life finds its focus and center in the practice of worship. As the 1971 Roman Catholic *General Instruction on the Liturgy of the Hours* (section 7) puts it, "the baptized, by regeneration and the anointing of the Holy Spirit, are consecrated into a spiritual house and a holy priesthood. They become capable of taking part in the worship of the New Testament, not thanks to themselves, but to the gift and merits of Christ."

If that worship is to be true to the priestly character of the Christian life and its participation in the priesthood of Christ, it should, therefore, have as its heart the offering of praise and of intercessory prayer—precisely the two elements which we have seen were at the heart of biblical and later "cathedral" patterns of prayer. Thus, the Letter to the Hebrews is able to go on to exhort its readers: "through him [i.e., Christ] then, let us continually offer up a sacrifice of praise to God, that is, the fruit of lips that confess [*homologounton*] his name" (Hebrews 13:15).

Thus, whenever we pray as Christians, we do not pray alone. We pray both through Christ and with Christ and in Christ, and Christ prays for us and with us and in us, so that, through the work of the Holy Spirit, our prayer becomes Christ's prayer and his prayer becomes our prayer. St. Augustine reflects this understanding when he writes: "When the body of the Son prays, it does not separate its Head from itself; and it is the one savior of his body, our Lord Jesus Christ, the Son of God, who prays for us, and prays in us, and is prayed to by us. He prays for us as our priest; he prays in us as our head; he is prayed to by us as our God. Let us therefore recognize our words in him and his words in us" (*Enarr. in Ps.* 85.1).

Yet, if this prayer is really to be priestly, both these activities—the offering of praise and of intercession—must necessarily be done for the sake of others. As J. G. Davies has said, a priesthood:

> is never established for itself, so that for the royal priesthood to celebrate its own *cultus* for its own needs is to deny its very *raison d'être*; it would cease in fact to function as a priesthood. An introverted *cultus* performed by the covenant people is therefore a contradiction of their office, a rejection of their commission and a failure to participate in the *missio Dei*. It makes nonsense of the whole idea of covenant and priesthood. This means that only a *cultus* which is outward looking and related to the world can be regarded as an authentic act of Christian worship. If it is not worldly, in this sense, then Christians are not exercising their baptismal priesthood.

Thus, we are called not merely to offer praise and thanksgiving for what God has done for each one of us individually, nor even for the church collectively, but to render to God the praise that is due from the whole of creation. Similarly, our intercession should be focused primarily not upon ourselves and our own needs, nor even just on that of other Christians, but rather upon the needs of the whole world for which Christ died and which he desires to be saved (see 1 Timothy 2:1-2). In this way, Christian prayer also has a strong eschatological dimension: it both prays for the coming of the kingdom of God, and is itself a foretaste of the heavenly praise that will be sung unceasingly before the throne of God and of the Lamb by "every creature in heaven and on earth and under the earth and in the sea" (Revelation 5:13).

Unfortunately, of course, this is exactly where much Christian worship tends to fall short of its ideal. Instead of this global vision of their vocation, Christians easily lapse into prayer that concentrates upon themselves and those near and dear to them. We offer praise and thanksgiving for the things for which we happen to feel grateful, but if such emotions are lacking, we have difficulty in articulating prayer of this sort at all. "Free intercessions" in church services generally produce a rush of requests for ecclesiastical concerns, for friends of the members of the congregation who are sick, and in some traditions for loved ones who have departed this life; but there is often a long and embarrassing silence when worshippers are asked to turn their attention to the wider community, to national, international or global issues—unless some major crisis has recently filled newspaper headlines. Moreover, it sometimes even happens that those who have been asked to lead intercessory prayer in a service will turn that activity instead into a meditation focused upon the spiritual relationship between the worshippers and God—and will be quite unaware that there is any difference between the two sorts of prayer.

The result is that much communal Christian worship, when left to the unfettered control of those leading it, becomes "monastic" rather than "cathedral" in character, and that much individual prayer does the same, or does not happen at all unless the emotions are stirred by particular feelings of gratitude or need.

The Obligation to Pray

The Christian obligation to engage in regular, daily prayer has often been presented as though it were some external rule laid upon the believer. Indeed, the choice of the terms *officium*, "duty," to describe the daily act of worship in ancient Western monastic rules, and of *pensum*, "task," to denote the prescribed number of psalms to be recited on each occasion in those services, is both a symptom of such an attitude, and an encouragement to its persistence. But from what has been said above, it should be clear that the obligation to pray is much deeper than that language would seem to imply: it springs from the very nature of our Christian vocation itself and is part of the privilege granted to those who are baptized to share in the continuing priestly ministry of Christ. It is a part of our stewardship of creation that we offer the sacrifice of praise on its behalf, and part of our responsibility for the salvation of all humankind that we intercede for the world.

This priestly vocation belongs equally to all members of the church—laity and clergy alike. In the course of history, however, this vision has become obscured by developments in both the "cathedral" and "monastic" traditions. The early "cathedral" tradition originally emphasized daily prayer as something that belonged to the church as a whole, and laid no particular obligation upon any one person to participate in it more than any other. Even if some individuals were absent, the prayer of the church would still go on, and the clergy only had a special responsibility to be there when it was their turn to exercise a particular ministry within the body. Monastic rules, on the other hand, insisted that each individual member of the community had to be present at every single prescribed time of prayer, or if that were not possible, to make up the prayer that was missed on his or her own. It was not enough that the rest of the community maintained that hour of prayer: if the individual did not participate in it, then he or she would derive no spiritual benefit from it.

Although the principles of "cathedral" and "monastic" prayer may thus appear to be in direct conflict with each other, in later centuries they were in fact combined in an unfortunate way. The result was that clergy and members of religious orders were required to adhere to the "monastic" rule of praying every prescribed office individually, without any omission; but at the same time it was thought that they alone could represent the church, and therefore that the presence of lay people was superfluous and added nothing to the efficacy of the church's prayer. However, while this particular combination of "cathedral" and "monastic" views of the obligation to pray may have produced unsatisfactory consequences, this does not mean that one must necessarily choose either one or the other alone. On the contrary, rightly understood, both have something to contribute to a more balanced view of the Christian obligation to pray.

The "cathedral" tradition correctly stresses that Christian prayer is something that is first and foremost the responsibility and privilege of the *laos*, the people of God as a whole, not of an individual. It thus acts as a counterbalance to a "monastic" tendency, which may lead the individual to think that if he or she happens to miss one or more times of prayer for one reason or another, then the prayer of the church has not taken place: it can, and does, go on without a particular individual. On the other hand, the "monastic" insistence on the importance of the individual's part in prayer can guard against taking the ecclesial aspect too far. Some Christians suppose that as long as someone does the church's praying, it does not matter whether they themselves ever pray at all. On the contrary, regular prayer is part of the vocation of every Christian, and not just of one particular group.

The role of the ordained minister, therefore, is not to do the Christian community's praying on its behalf, but to lead that community in regular prayer, and to enable and encourage the prayer of the church to take place. This is a much more demanding obligation than vicarious praying, and involves teaching people how to pray as well as making the practical arrangements for the occasions of communal prayer and for individuals to share in it in some way even when they are unable to be physically present. And because ordained ministers are the ones who preside over the whole life of the Christian community, they are the appropriate persons to preside over the community's gatherings for prayer—just they normally preside over its celebration of the sacraments and other public acts of worship—so that it may be more clearly seen that this is indeed the church at prayer. It perhaps needs to be emphasized, however, that this presiding role does not prevent others from exercising their particular ministerial gifts in leading the praises and prayers of the people within the gathering, nor does it preclude others from presiding in the absence of an ordained minister.

Communal Prayer

The ecclesiological aspect of Christian prayer naturally receives its fullest liturgical expression when believers assemble together to pray, and so manifest the presence both of Christ ("When two or three are gathered in my name, I am there among them" Matthew 18:20) and also of the church. Corporate daily prayer, therefore, is not an optional extra; it is what all Christian prayer is meant to be. There is, strictly speaking, no such thing as private prayer for a Christian. Whenever we pray, we do so as a member of the body of Christ and united by the Spirit with the whole company of earth and heaven. We pray as the church and with the church.

Nevertheless, there are inevitably times when Christians are unable to join physically with others in the regular worship of God, and so must pray on their own. Here the use of common forms of prayer becomes very important. Through participation in patterns of prayer that are being used by other members of the church, the individual believers are reminded of the ecclesial character of all Christian praying and are helped to shape their prayers according to the intrinsic spirit of their priestly commission.

THE FREQUENCY OF PRAYER

How often should one pray? Historical precedents exist within the Christian tradition for almost any pattern of prayer that one might imagine—twice a day (morning and evening), three times a day (morning, noon, and evening), five times a day (by adding 9:00 A.M. and 3:00 P.M. to the former hours, following the principal divisions of the day in the ancient Roman empire), seven times a day (to correspond with what is said in Ps. 119:164), and so on. There have even been communities that attempted to pray at every single hour of the day and night.

Thus, no one arrangement can claim absolute authority by reference to the tradition. Even the practice of prayer twice a day, morning and evening, only becomes clearly evidenced from the fourth century onward. Prior to that time prayer at least three times a day seems to have been a more common custom, together with a time of prayer during the night. In their desire to restore what they view as the practice of the early church, modern liturgical revisers have usually ignored prayer during the night, but there is no sign that early Christians regarded it as any less important than times of prayer during the day. Indeed, prayer at night had a particular significance for them in their vigilance for the return of Christ in glory, for they knew that "the day of the Lord will come like a thief in the night" (1 Thessalonians 5:2; see also Matthew 24:43; 25:6; Mark 13:35; Luke 12:38-40; 2 Peter 3:10; Revelation 3:3; 16:15). Of course, rising to pray in the middle of the night was not nearly as demanding in a culture where there was little to do except sleep between sunset and sunrise as it would be for modern Christians.

Yet, in spite of the specific patterns of prayer that they urged people to adopt, early Christian writers were quite convinced that there was only one absolute rule, that one should pray "without ceasing," following St Paul's injunction (1 Thessalonians 5:17). As we have seen, however, "cathedral" and "monastic" traditions interpreted this differently, the former understanding it to mean that one's whole life should become an act of worship offered to God, the latter that one should try to spend as much time as possible in actual prayer. As well as being impractical for most people to follow, the "monastic" interpretation, if taken too seriously, implies a wholly negative attitude toward the world, as irrelevant and even hostile to the spiritual life. While in one sense it is true that we can never pray too often, because we are easily inclined to forget God in our daily lives and need constant reminders, yet our Christian duty often requires us to focus all our attention on the tasks that lie before us and not to be distracted from them by pious thoughts. As a former Archbishop of Canterbury, William Temple, once said, "in order to serve God properly, there are times when we must forget him."

Thus, for most Christians some pattern of regular prayer at set times is necessary, whatever that pattern may be. And since Christian prayer is not an individual activity but a participation in the prayer of the church, then the pattern ought to be one which is set by the church and not merely by the individual. This does not necessarily mean that all Christians throughout the world need to pray at exactly the same moments, but it does mean that Christians need at least to associate themselves with a larger ecclesial group (for example, a congregation, a diocese, or a denomination) in the times of day at which they pray as well as in the forms of worship that they use.

SUGGESTIONS FOR FURTHER READING

Bradshaw, Paul F. "Daily Prayer," in Kenneth Stevenson & Bryan Spinks, eds., *The Identity of Anglican Worship*. London: Mowbrays, 1991. Pp. 69-79.

Davies, J.G. *Worship and Mission*. London: SCM Press, 1966.

Jungmann, Joseph. *The Place of Christ in Liturgical Prayer*. London: Chapman, 1965.

Salmon, Pierre. *The Breviary through the Centuries*. Collegeville, Minn.: Liturgical Press, 1962.

5

PSALMS AND PRAYER

Although the canonical psalms have been a major component of Christian worship throughout its history, many people still appear to be very unsure what it exactly is that they are supposed to be doing when they are asked to say or sing them: are all these words that we are reciting actually directed toward God—and do we really want to address to God some of the sentiments contained in them? Nor does knowledge of the complex history of their use and interpretation necessarily solve our problems and immediately make sense of the customs that we have inherited from the past. On the other hand, what historical understanding can do is to offer us some guidance in making decisions as to what are and are not appropriate ways for Christians to make use of the psalms in relation to their prayers.

PSALMS IN THE NEW TESTAMENT: PROPHECY OF THE MESSIAH

The book of Psalms is cited in the New Testament more often than any other Old Testament writing, and so it is obvious that the first Christians valued it very highly indeed. They had four principal beliefs about the nature of the psalms, which were perpetuated by Christians of later centuries: first, that they had been written by king David himself; second, that in so doing, he had been specially inspired by the Holy Spirit; third, that the psalms were to be understood as prophecy, like the writings of Isaiah, Jeremiah, and the other canonical prophets—indeed, as *the* prophetic work *par excellence*; and fourth, that their prophecy was essentially messianic or christological in focus. The verses of the psalms either spoke about the Messiah, or were addressed to the Messiah, or were the words of the Messiah.

Mark 12:35-37 provides us with an excellent example of all four of these beliefs. Here Jesus cites the first verse of Psalm 110, which he claims was written by David under the inspiration of the Holy Spirit, and he treats it as a prophecy about a future messiah:

> While Jesus was teaching in the temple, he said,
> "How can the scribes say that the Messiah is the son of David?
> David himself, by the Holy Spirit, declared,
>   'The Lord said to my Lord,
>   "Sit at my right hand,
>   until I put your enemies under your feet."'
> David himself calls him Lord; so how is he his son?"

We can see a similar use of the psalms in Acts 2:25-28, where in Peter's speech on the day of Pentecost, Psalm16.8-11 is quoted and interpreted as a messianic prophecy about Jesus.

These examples suggest that the psalms had an important place in early Christian preaching. Yet in spite of that, when it came to their use in worship, no special preference appears to have been accorded to these canonical texts over noncanonical ones. The first few generations of believers seem to have been just as happy to use their own compositions as those from the psalter, or even to mingle the two together. Thus in Acts 4:24-30, we find a quotation from Psalm 2 incorporated into a prayer, which interprets it christologically. Similarly, in a description of a Christian supper or *agape* by a North African Christian, Tertullian, at the end of the second century, he tells how after the meal "each is invited to stand in the middle and sing a hymn to God, from the holy scriptures or of his own composition as he is able" (*Apol.* 39). The fact that people are capable of doing this, he says, proves how little drinking goes on at such meals, contrary to the false accusations of revelry made by outsiders.

Tertullian's account parallels 1 Corinthians 14:26, where among the different verbal contributions that an individual may bring to the Christian assembly is a "hymn" (*psalmos*), which could mean either a canonical psalm or a noncanonical composition. We should also note

Ephesians 5:19, where believers are said to address one another "in psalms and hymns and spiritual songs." There are signs that a similar practice of composing religious songs for use in communal gatherings may have been the case in some contemporary Jewish circles.

There is no evidence to suggest, however, that any more than certain selected psalms, probably mainly those in which christological prophecy could easily be seen, were ever used in the worship of the first Christians, and certainly nothing to support the notion that the whole psalter was read through in its entirety. Furthermore, there is no evidence at all that the whole psalter was used in Jewish worship at that period, or even that any of the canonical psalms had yet attained a permanent place in the synagogue liturgy, and in later Jewish worship only about half of them have ever been used. The claim frequently made, therefore, that in saying the psalms we are praying the prayers that Jesus himself used, lacks any sure foundation. If we did want to imitate the words of Jesus in daily prayer, we would be on much safer ground if we recited the *Shema* ("Hear, O Israel, the LORD is our God, the LORD alone . . ." Deuteronomy 6:4-9), which many Jews of his time would have said twice daily but which the early church apparently abandoned very quickly, probably because its strong monotheistic tone did not have the right feel for a community moving toward a trinitarian faith.

PSALMS IN THE "CATHEDRAL" TRADITION: HYMNS AND PRAYERS

As we can see from the passages cited above, the primary context for the earliest Christian use of psalms in worship seems to have been occasional communal gatherings, and especially those involving meals, where individuals sang them to the others, who listened in silence or perhaps responded to each verse with a refrain. By the third century, however, we see signs of the beginning of an extension of this practice to other times of prayer. Tertullian tells us that the more assiduous worshippers included in their regular prayers those psalms containing an Alleluia, which others present would use as a response (*De or.* 27), thereby clearly implying that the rest as yet did not do this.

By the fourth century this custom had become a standard part of "cathedral" worship. Psalms 148-150, which were all "Alleluia" psalms, quickly came to form the nucleus of the praise element in the daily morning office everywhere. Psalm 51, which was ideally suited as an expression of penitence, was used as the first prayer of the day in many places (though this development may have come about as the result of the influence of the strongly penitential character of much monastic worship). Other psalms were included because of references in them to particular times of the day or night. Not surprisingly, for example, Psalm 141, with its reference in verse 2 to "the lifting up of my hands as an evening sacrifice," is found in virtually all Eastern evening offices, although not so clearly evidenced in the West, where at least in some areas part of Psalm 104 (see verses 19-23) seems to have been used instead. Psalm 63 was also part of the morning office in many places, because in the Greek translation of the psalms that was used by many early Christians verse 1 included the word "early" and verse 6 the phrase "in the mornings."

Several things need to be noted about the use of psalms in the "cathedral" tradition. First, it was still just as selective as the earlier use appears to have been, and perhaps even more so: only a very few psalms were incorporated into the "cathedral" office, and most of these were repeated every single day. Second, they were not chosen for their christological content but because of their suitability as Christian hymns and prayers. It may well be that some of the psalms used in Christian worship in earlier times were also selected on a similar basis, even though our New Testament evidence is strongest with regard to those psalms subject to christological interpretation. Third, in spite of their role as hymns or prayers, the psalms still function in a way as God's word addressed to human beings, and not just as the words of human beings addressed to God: for the most part they are performed responsorially, that is, with a cantor singing the verses to the people and the congregation responding with a refrain after each one—and it is that refrain, rather than the psalm itself, which expresses their praise of God. The refrain was not restricted to "Alleluia" alone, but could be composed of a verse chosen from the psalm. The significance of participating in the refrain was underlined by John Chrysostom:

> Do not then think that you have come here simply to say the
> words, but when you make the response, consider that
> response to be a covenant. For when you say, "Like the hart
> desires the watersprings, my soul desires you, O God," you
> make a covenant with God. You have signed a contract without

paper or ink; you have confessed with your voice that you love him more than all, that you prefer nothing to him, and that you burn with love for him. (*Expos. in Ps.* 41.5).

Finally, there is now a clear dominance of biblical texts over nonbiblical material, which came about as the result of the need to combat heresy: since heretical groups were propagating their beliefs through the medium of their hymns, other Christians began to view all noncanonical compositions with considerable suspicion. The only sure way for them to avoid unwittingly uttering heretical sentiments, therefore, seemed to be to restrict themselves to songs taken from the scriptures, which, as the inspired word of God, were free from all taint of distrust. St. Basil, for example, contrasts the canonical psalms as "the songs of the Spirit" with ecclesiastical compositions, which he describes as "the words of mere humans" (*Ep.* 207.4). Consequently, only a very few well established noncanonical hymns—most notably *Gloria in excelsis* ("Glory to God in the highest") and *Phos hilaron* ("O Gladsome Light")—survived in later usage from what must formerly have been an enormous wealth of creative contributions.

PSALMS IN THE "MONASTIC" TRADITION: THE WHOLE PSALTER

As we saw in the first chapter, the primary aim of early "monastic" prayer was spiritual growth, to seek to conform one's life more and more to Christ. Since the psalms had traditionally been understood as being christological in character, and written under the special inspiration of the Holy Spirit, what better way could there be to become more Christ-like than to meditate on the words of the psalms, and allow their sentiments to shape one's spirituality? It is not surprising, therefore, that psalms soon assumed the central position in the worship of most monastic communities. In some ways this might perhaps be described as a continuation of the practice of earlier times. What was certainly an innovation, however, was the extension of the christological interpretation to encompass the whole 150 psalms and the use of them all in regular daily worship, often in their biblical sequence without any regard for their appropriateness to specific hours and occasions. As one might imagine, this step involved quite strained exegesis of some texts in order to find a christological aspect.

Characteristic of the classical "monastic" use was the alternation of psalm and silence, whether recited by individuals alone during their daily labors, by groups of ascetics gathered together informally, or by organized communities in their regular times of prayer. Here, one person would read or chant the verses of the psalm while others present listened, and then there would follow a period of silent reflection on the word of God and interior prayer for spiritual growth—sometimes being concluded with the Lord's Prayer or a collect—before the next psalm was recited.

This meditative usage did not at first usually involve any refrain or other corporate response to the psalm. However, some monastic communities introduced the responsorial method of performing the psalms, doubtless influenced by the "cathedral" tradition. Moreover, in an effort to alleviate monotony and boredom in the longer night vigils, they frequently alternated groups of psalms chanted responsorially with groups that involved a variation of this method, known as antiphonal psalmody. In this latter usage, the congregation was divided into two choirs and took it in turns to sing the refrain to the verses sung by the soloist, or sometimes by two soloists alternating the verses.

LATER DEVELOPMENTS: THE TRADITIONS COMBINED

As we saw in Chapter 2, in later centuries monastic communities in the West began to adopt a "cathedral" interpretation of their daily offices in place of the earlier "monastic" one. The result as far as psalmody was concerned was a fusion of the two traditions. On the one hand, the principle of the use of the whole psalter and its christological interpretation were retained from the "monastic" tradition, while on the other hand the idea that the psalms constituted the church's hymns of praise was appropriated from the "cathedral" tradition.

This development had a number of consequences. It meant that all psalms, regardless of their contents, had to be understood as somehow bringing praise to God. This was done by the claim that God liked to hear them, and it resulted in the belief that it was the chanting of the psalm itself—rather than the response made to the verses—that glorified God, so that the psalms ceased to be seen as God's word addressed to the worshippers and were viewed instead as the voice of the church to God. This in turn gave rise to a change in the method of antiphonal psalmody described earlier: the two choirs themselves, instead of a soloist, began to sing the verses alternately, and the refrain (or antiphon as it came to be called) was relegated to the beginning and end of the whole psalm. Moreover, the *Gloria Patri*, "Glory be to the Father . . .," was now added as a doxological conclusion to antiphonal psalmody, though not to the older responsorial psalmody. Finally, the period of silence between the psalms declined in importance and eventually disappeared altogether, since it was no longer seen as an essential element in the appropriation of the psalm. In short, the psalms were no longer used *in* Christian prayer but *as* Christian prayer.

In this way the cycle of 150 psalms, interpreted christologically and understood as the church's praise, came to dominate both spiritual formation and the patterns of daily worship for religious communities and also for individuals who sought to imitate their life. But because of the powerful influence that monasticism exerted on the Christian tradition, this practice extended further still and ultimately shaped both the public services of the church and Western spirituality in general, thus creating a legacy that remains with us to this day.

Some Lessons from History

1. *The Christian tradition does not require that only the canonical psalms and biblical canticles be used in worship.* As we have seen, prior to the fourth century no special status seems to have been given in Christian worship to canonical compositions over noncanonical ones. Moreover, even though the fourth-century "back to the Bible" movement led to the almost complete disappearance of a wealth of early Christian hymns, we need to note that this phase did not last, but the trend was slowly reversed in later centuries, with hymnic additions often at first being grafted onto scriptural texts as commentary and interpretation of them and then later being added to them as independent compositions or even entirely substituted for them.

The process was repeated at the time of the Reformation, when once again the great medieval flowering of hymnody was looked upon with deep distrust by many of the Reformers, who saw it as harboring erroneous doctrine and preferred to return to the safety of *sola scriptura*, scripture alone. While Luther was content merely to base many of the German hymns that he wrote upon psalms, the psalter itself—albeit in metrical version—became the hymn book of the Reformed tradition. But once again such scriptural purity did not last. Many metrical versions became instead paraphrases of the original psalm, introducing an element of subjective interpretation and sometimes explicit Christianization to the text, as for example in the version of Psalm 72 by Isaac Watts (1674-1748), which begins, "Jesus shall reign where'er the sun/Doth his successive journeys run." Eventually hymns having only a tenuous connection with biblical passages made an appearance alongside the traditional metrical psalms, and often displaced them altogether.

These examples of oscillation in the use of scriptural material as hymns and prayers reflect an inevitable tension within Christian experience. The church on the one hand wants to affirm fidelity to the biblical foundation of the faith, but on the other hand constantly needs to interpret that faith in relation to contemporary culture and spirituality. While Christian liturgy should certainly always strive to be biblical in character, this does not mean that the contents of our worship must necessarily be limited to biblical texts alone. We can supplement them with appropriate non-canonical compositions, whether ancient or modern.

2. *The Christian tradition does not require that the whole psalter be used in worship.* Prior to the monastic movement in the fourth century, Christians seem to have used only a small number of appropriate psalms in their worship, and hence there is nothing improper about Christians today being selective in our approach to the psalter. This does not necessarily mean that the fewer psalms we use the better, nor do we have to imitate the fourth-century "cathedral" office and repeat the same psalms every single day. We have been given a rich heritage of psalmody, and there is no reason why we should not make extensive use of it. But we are not obliged to employ every one of the psalms, nor to work through them within a defined period of time. We may decide to repeat some psalms frequently, even daily, in order to establish rhythm and stability in our prayer; we may choose to use others less often, restricting them just to those occasions when they seem appropriate; and we may opt to use others only very rarely or not at all.

It must be admitted that some will raise the objection that such subjectivism in the use of the psalter is improper: we ought to accept the psalms just as they are presented to us in the Bible and not pick and choose the ones that we happen to like and discard the rest. However, since this issue is part of the larger question of how we use scripture in worship, it will not be addressed here, but in the next chapter.

3. *Psalms can have more than just one meaning or interpretation*. Twentieth-century biblical scholarship has made it difficult to perpetuate the traditional christological interpretation of the psalter, since scholars now reject not only the Davidic authorship of the psalms but also the idea that their authors intended them to be prophetic compositions at all, still less that they were meant to be about a future messiah. Thus today we understand the psalms in a very different way from earlier generations, and this creates an apparent contradiction between our intellectual perception of the text and the devotional tradition of its use.

Yet is it true that the only legitimate interpretation of a biblical text is the meaning that its author originally intended when writing it? Is it not possible for a text to have several possible meanings, of which author's is only one? After all, we accept this approach in relation to other texts and artistic creations. Although it may considerably increase our understanding and appreciation to be told what a poet or artist originally intended in creating a poem or work of art, that does not mean that we are not allowed to interpret the work in any other way or discover any other significance in it. For example, people can derive a great deal from a performance of *Hamlet* without knowing anything at all about the historical details of the Danes or about William Shakespeare's own intentions in writing the play.

Surely, then, what is permissible in the case of other literary and artistic works is also legitimate in the case of biblical material. In any case, with some scriptural texts, and especially the psalms, it is often impossible to know what the original context of their composition was or what the author might have intended. Moreover, within the Bible itself, texts are frequently subjected to reinterpretation by the incorporation of earlier material from another milieu within a later work with a different focus. In such a situation, what constitutes the "author's original intent"? Is it the purpose that the writers of the various component parts had when they were first set down or the meaning given to the material by its final compiler or redactor?

Certainly, the more recent adoption by biblical scholars of other approaches to literary criticism, such as that of Paul Ricoeur, would lend support to the notion of multiple meanings, and movements like canonical criticism and reader-response criticism follow a similar path. This opens up the possibility, therefore, that individual psalms may have several equally legitimate interpretations, depending upon the particular context in which they are used. We must certainly try to take into account their original meaning, where that can be discovered, but we are not limited to that as the only true meaning. A traditional christological interpretation of a psalm is thus not ruled out. On the other hand, we are not justified in going to the other extreme and claiming that the christological interpretation is the true meaning of the psalm: it remains as one way among others in which a psalm may be understood.

4. *Every psalm does not have to be interpreted in exactly the same way.* As we have seen, after the fourth century there developed a tendency to regard all psalms as being fundamentally alike and to use them indifferently, without paying any attention to whether they expressed praise or lamentation; whether they referred to morning, evening, or night; or whether they were appropriate to the particular season of the liturgical year. This implies that psalms can be made to mean almost anything at all that we want them to mean, and such a conclusion creates a major stumbling block for their use today. Words and phrases may be capable of a wide range of meanings, but they are not infinitely elastic; and ordinary people's common sense often rightly prevents them accepting an interpretation that seems to overstep the boundaries of a legitimate reading of the text. Much of the difficulty with the christological interpretation of psalms, for example, arises from a strained and artificial attempt to force far too many psalms into this particular mold and not from a fundamental rejection of the whole idea of viewing certain psalms in that way. The same problem is created when people are informed that, though a psalm may seem to be an attack upon one's enemies, it is really a hymn of praise to God.

We need rather to distinguish between different sorts of psalms and use them according to their individual contents, whether as hymns of praise, as prayers, as christological poems, or as scriptural lections.

While some psalms naturally lend themselves to appropriation as the hymns and prayers of the Christian community (as, for example, Psalms 51, 148-150), and can be used in this way together with other scriptural canticles or noncanonical hymns and prayers, other psalms are less suitable for use on the lips of Christians to address to God. What, for example, are we to do with Psalm 22 ("My God, my God, why have you forsaken me?") or Psalm 110 ("The LORD says to my lord, 'Sit at my right hand, until I make your enemies your footstool'"). Both these have been so colored by a christological reading within the New Testament itself and ever since that it is really quite impossible to detach them from that interpretation. Such psalms as these should not be employed as though they were our words addressed to God, but rather as God's word addressed to us. The same is also true of a number of other psalms that do not lend themselves to christological interpretation. Psalm 37, for instance ("Do not fret because of the wicked; do not be envious of wrongdoers"), may contain much that is valuable and true about the human relationship to God, but it is hardly an appropriate vehicle for expressing direct praise or petition. These psalms can certainly still find a place in Christian worship, but as a part of a ministry of the Word, to which worshippers may respond either with a vocal refrain or with a period of silent meditation.

In this way, the canonical psalms can still offer a rich treasury on which we may draw for our prayer life, providing that we do not attempt to use them alone, that we do not attempt to use them all, and that we do use them intelligently and in accordance with the sense of their contents, rather than some predetermined interpretative principle—whether, theological, liturgical, or musical. For in the words of St Paul—which the early monastic fathers were fond of quoting—"I will sing praise with the spirit, but I will sing praise with the mind also" (1 Corinthians 14:15).

SUGGESTIONS FOR FURTHER READING

Bradshaw, Paul F. "From Word to Action: The Changing Role of Psalmody in Early Christianity," in Martin Dudley, ed. *Like a Two-Edged Sword: The Word of God in Liturgy and History*. Norwich: Canterbury Press, 1995. Pp. 21-37.

Brueggemann, Walter. *The Message of the Psalms*. Minneapolis: Augsburg Press, 1984.

Daley, Brian. "Is Patristic Exegesis still Usable? Reflections on Early Christian Interpretation of the Psalms," *Communio* 29 (2002): 185-216.

Eaton, John. *The Psalms: a Historical and Spiritual Commentary*. London: T & T Clark, 2003.

Fischer, Balthasar. "Christ in the Psalms," *Theology Digest* 1 (1951): 53-57.

Holladay, William L. *The Psalms through Three Thousand Years*. Minneapolis: Fortress Press 1992.

McKinnon, James W. "On the Question of Psalmody in the Ancient Synagogue," *Early Music History* 6 (1986): 159-191.

Ricoeur, Paul. *Essays on Biblical Interpretation*. Philadelphia: Fortress Press, 1980.

Salmon, Pierre. *The Breviary through the Centuries*. Collegeville, Minn.: Liturgical Press, 1962. Chap. 3.

6

BIBLE READING AND PRAYER

Most Christians take for granted the presence of one or more biblical readings in church services, and hardly ever give any thought to why they are there, or what their function might be in relation to the rest of the act of worship. Moreover, it may appear at first sight that whenever there is a reading from scripture, the same activity must be going on each time. But appearances can be misleading, and it may well be that such readings are fulfilling quite different functions in different contexts. In particular, Bible readings have a quite different role in relation to "cathedral" prayer than they do in relation to "monastic" prayer.

"MONASTIC" PRAYER AND A DIDACTIC MINISTRY OF THE WORD

Although it may not always be drawn from the Bible, a reading of some sort is an almost indispensable element of "monastic" prayer, since it constitutes the source of inspiration for the meditation and prayer that follow.

We can see this clearly in the forms of daily prayer which evolved within the fourth-century monastic communities in the Egyptian desert. In the Pachomian communities of Upper (southern) Egypt, it appears that passages from scripture were read aloud by different members of the community in turn at the morning and evening assemblies each day, and between each reading was a period for silent reflection and prayer. In the monastic communities of Lower (northern) Egypt, on the other hand, whatever John Cassian claims to have observed, evidence points to communal gatherings for worship only on Saturdays and Sundays. During the rest of the week the brothers prayed individually in their cells, and seem to have used the canonical psalms alone as the food for their daily prayer, alternating each psalm with a time of silent meditation.

It was this pattern of psalms and prayer which monastic communities in other parts of the world would later take up as the heart of their daily assemblies for worship, often concluding each period of silent prayer with either the Lord's Prayer or an appropriate collect. Scripture reading itself had a much less prominent part, apart of course from its place in the celebration of the Eucharist. In the principal Western monastic traditions, for example, it is only in the long night offices that we find substantial Bible readings. At the other hours of the day any readings that there were tended to be very brief indeed, often recited from memory rather than read from a book, and placed at the conclusion of the main psalmody of the office, prior to the final prayers.

Such a use of the scriptures, including the psalms, might well be described as pedagogical or formational, since its original intent was to further the individual's spiritual growth. Whether the texts were recited from memory by one person alone or read aloud in a community, the purpose was basically the same: that those who heard might become acquainted with the contents of the biblical books, or deepen their existing knowledge of them, so as to enrich their understanding and shape their lives in the light of them. This kind of reading is really nothing else but Bible study, and for that reason we have chosen to call it a didactic ministry of the Word.

This way of using scripture in worship, however, is not restricted to early monasticism, but forms part of a long tradition of the educational function of Bible reading in this context. It seems, for example, that the origins of the Jewish synagogue liturgy may lie in the regular reading of portions of the Law, sabbath by sabbath, to which other acts of prayer that had become an individual daily obligation were eventually joined. This public reading of the Law, together with its interpretation by those who were learned in it, was intended to instill a knowledge of God's will in the hearers, and stir them up to obey it.

The same motive would also seem to lie behind the inclusion of a formal ministry of the Word in the early Christian eucharistic rite described by Justin Martyr in the second century: "The records of the apostles or the writings of the prophets are read for as long as time allows. Then, when the reader has finished, the president in a discourse admonishes and exhorts [us] to imitate these good things" (*1 Apol.* 67.3-5; English translation from R.C.D. Jasper and G.J. Cuming, *Prayers of the Eucharist: Early and Reformed* [London: Collins, 1975], pp. 19-20). This Sunday ministry of the Word seems to have been part of a more extensive pattern of regular Bible study in the early Christian community, for Tertullian at the end of the second century speaks of services of the Word also being held on Wednesdays and Fridays every week at the ninth hour, about 3 P.M. (*De ieiun.* 10; *De cult. fem.* 2.11). This practice still persisted in the fourth century: the ecclesiastical historian Socrates states that in Alexandria "on Wednesdays and Fridays the scriptures are read, and the teachers interpret them" (*Hist. eccl.* 5.22), and Egeria records that at Jerusalem it was the custom for there to be multiple sermons by any presbyters who wished, as well as by the bishop, at the Sunday, Wednesday, and Friday services (25.1; 26.1; 27.6; 43.2)—a practice confirmed by other sources from the same period as also existing in other Eastern churches.

Several characteristics help us distinguish this didactic type from other forms of the ministry of the word. First, as we have seen, the readings tend to be followed either by a homily or explanation, or alternatively by a period of silence in which the meaning of the words is internalized, or sometimes by both of these. Second, any preaching is directed primarily toward the application of the scriptures to the life of the individual, rather than, for instance, to the occasion being celebrated or to the common life of the community. Moreover, any vocalized prayer that is closely related to the ministry of the Word will tend to have the character of petition for such spiritual growth. Third, although the event may also include other elements of worship, these tend not be related to the ministry of the Word, which is seen as fulfilling its purpose not by preparing people in some way for the external action of the rest of the rite but by exercising an internal effect upon their spiritual formation.

A further common tendency is for the readings to be arranged on the basis of what is termed by scholars *lectio continua,* "continuous reading"—that is, the passages read on successive occasions follow sequentially through the same book of the Bible, in order that its contents may be laid out thoroughly and systematically. The 1560 *Book of Discipline* of the Church of Scotland, for example, judged this to be the correct way to organize biblical readings:

> We think it most expedient that the Scriptures be read in order, that is, that some one book of the Old and the New Testament be begun and orderly read to the end. And the same we judge of preaching, where the Minister for most part remaineth in one place: for this skipping and divagation from place to place of the Scripture, be it in reading, or be it in preaching, we judge not so profitable to edify the Church, as the continual following of one text. (From David Laing, ed., *The Works of John Knox*, vol.2 [Edinburgh, 1855], pp. 240-41. Spellings have been modernized.)

Of course, such public reading of the canonical texts was really the only practical way in ages past for most people to engage in Bible study. Before the invention of movable type in the mid-fifteenth century, it would have been difficult to procure multiple copies of the scriptures within a community; and before the advances in printing technology in the nineteenth century, which for the first time enabled the mass production of books at a reasonable cost, it would have been much too expensive to do so. In any case, although levels of literacy among ordinary people did begin to rise from the time of the Renaissance onward, it was really not until the emergence of more widespread formal education in the nineteenth century that the majority would have been able to make use of such texts anyway. It will therefore be apparent that the exhortations to study the Bible at home found in a number of ancient Christian writings can only have been possible for a relatively few educated and wealthier members of the church.

The situation today, however, is very different—at least in the regions of the world where wealth and education are more plentiful; and in these places it has become possible for ordinary people, and not just an elite, to meditate on biblical texts and other spiritual writings entirely on their own. Nevertheless, even in such circumstances, there is still some abiding value in encouraging this activity to continue to take place in a communal context as well, so that the thoughts and ideas that are generated within the minds of individual participants can be shared with, and tested by, other members of the Christian community.

"CATHEDRAL" PRAYER AND AN ANAMNETIC MINISTRY OF THE WORD

One of the principal features of the classic forms of the "cathedral" office, in contrast to "monastic" prayer, is the complete absence of a ministry of the Word from the daily services. On the other hand, as we have indicated earlier, the psalmody itself can be viewed as constituting a form of ministry of the Word, with the verses being chanted by a cantor to the congregation, which responds with a refrain repeated after each one. The responsorial psalm within the eucharistic ministry of the Word, which is also evidenced from the fourth century onward and forms a parallel to this use in the office, was certainly understood as constituting one of the readings. Both practices seem to have their roots in the informal ministry of the Word described in 1 Corinthians 14:26, where different members of the Christian community bring "a hymn, a lesson, a revelation, a tongue, or an interpretation," and in the practice alluded to in Ephesians 5:19, where believers are said to address one another in "psalms and hymns and spiritual songs."

There is, however, an even clearer illustration of the distinctive way in which scripture was used in relation to prayer in the early "cathedral" tradition, and that is the Sunday vigil service, which apparently originated in fourth-century Jerusalem but soon spread elsewhere. Held early each Sunday morning, the day of Christ's resurrection, in the very place where that event was believed to have happened, its climax was the reading of the same passage of scripture every single week—the account of the passion and resurrection of Christ. Clearly what was going on here was something very different from a didactic ministry of the Word. Even the most dull-witted Jerusalem worshipper must have become thoroughly familiar with the contents of the reading after the first few months of such frequent use. Its purpose, therefore, was not simply to advance people's knowledge of the Bible, but to provide the biblical warrant and foundation for the liturgical rite being celebrated. The whole rite was a liturgical remembrance (*anamnesis*) of Christ's resurrection, and the Gospel reading played a central part in that, recalling the act of God that lay behind it and interpreting the meaning of what was going on.

There are few extant precedents for this sort of anamnetic use of scripture in the Christian tradition prior to the fourth century, partially because fixed lectionary prescriptions had not yet begun to be recorded but chiefly because the liturgical year had hardly begun to evolve, and it was really the gradual institution of feasts and special occasions that led to the expansion of this way of reading the Bible in worship. We can, however, see rudimentary forms of it in ancient Israelite religion in the injunctions to say a word of explanation in connection with the Passover and the offering of firstfruits (Exodus 12:26-27; Deuteronomy 26:5-10), and an early Christian development in the readings of the Paschal vigil, which are thematic in content. But it is really from the fourth century onward that it begins to flower, as various Christian festivals and special occasions begin to emerge and are assigned readings that relate to the particular celebration and interpret its meaning.

Such a liturgy of the Word will necessarily involve selective readings rather than *lectio continua*. Usually no attempt is made to ensure that every psalm or passage of scripture is read at some point in the course of the liturgical year, and the readings will often, though not always, be shorter than those of a didactic ministry of the Word. The readings may, or may not, be followed by a homily or other explanation; but both they and the homily, where there is one, will always be closely related to the rest of the liturgical rite with regard to their themes and content, because they serve as a commentary on it and as a stimulus or springboard for the response of praise and prayer.

Whatever the theory, the boundaries between these two types of ministry of the Word will inevitably be somewhat blurred in actual practice. An anamnetic ministry of the Word will exercise a didactic function for those who are unfamiliar with the tradition, and readings that were at first intended to be didactic can in the course of time become anamnetic, as they grow in familiarity to the hearers and become associated with particular occasions. It may be argued, for example, that this is in large part what happened to the Sunday eucharistic lectionary in both East and West.

What ultimately distinguishes the didactic from the anamnetic, however, is not so much the original intention of those who organized the readings, nor even the external arrangement or structure of the ministry of the Word, but the primary function that the lections themselves currently exercise. Are they principally aimed at the education and formation of the individual members of the assembled community, with only a loose or non-existent connection with the rest of the liturgical rite? Or, on the contrary, are they intimately related to the meaning of what is being celebrated, interpreting and stimulating the liturgical action itself? If we have difficulty in seeing answers to these questions in relation to specific instances of the ministry of the Word that we experience today, that problem may explain why we have some confusion over what biblical readings are supposed to be doing in our contemporary liturgies.

A Canon Within the Canon?

Some will object on principle to the selective use of psalms or other parts of scripture in an anamnetic ministry of the Word. Is this not the creation of a subjective canon within the canon? Ought we not rather to read the Word of God exactly as it is given to us?

At first sight, this argument may appear to have some force. However, it can really only be sustained by those who recite every single verse of every single psalm in worship, and who read every single word of the Bible in their lectionaries; and it would be hard to find any Christian today who does that. Once a person has eliminated as little as one biblical verse from use in worship, he or she has admitted to engaging in subjective selection. Even the arrangement of a lectionary—deciding what readings are to be read upon what occasion, and which Old Testament reading to put alongside a New Testament reading, or which psalm should accompany them—involves subjective judgment and interpretation. It is impossible get away from it. Thus, although it may appear that the argument is about the *principle* of an objective rather than a subjective use of scripture, in fact it turns out that all parties are agreed that some subjectivism is possible, and the discussion is only about the legitimate degree of subjectivism—a very different matter indeed.

At this point it may be helpful to consider a distinction between reading the Bible for the purposes of study on the one hand, and its proclamation as liturgical *anamnesis* on the other. All scripture may indeed be "useful for teaching, for reproof, for correction, and for training in righteousness" (2 Timothy 3:16). But while all things are lawful, not everything is helpful or builds up (1 Corinthians 10:23). Thus, although it is right for Christians to retain a commitment to the whole Bible as scripture and to employ it fully for the purposes of study and even, if desired, as a basis for meditation and "monastic" prayer, yet not every biblical passage is equally fruitful in recalling God's saving works so that worshippers may be moved to offer praise and intercession or helped to make sense of the rites that they are celebrating. Some parts of the Bible lend themselves far more easily to this function than others. For this end, therefore, a selective and carefully organized lectionary would be far more beneficial than simply reading through biblical books sucessively in the course of regular worship. In some contexts, all that may be needed is as little as a single verse; in others, a somewhat longer extract, or a group of extracts related to one another, will be required.

In abstracting scriptural texts in this way, however, great care needs to be taken to avoid going too far and destroying the integrity of the original either by an insensitive wrenching of individual verses from their proper context or by employing passages in senses at variance with their meaning in their original setting. Unfortunately, both these mistakes were frequently made in traditional appropriations of scripture in worship, and so have provided infelicitous precedents, which liturgical revisers of today are often all too willing to follow uncritically. This happened not only in the selection of readings and psalms to be used in worship but also in the manner in which biblical phrases were incorporated into Christian hymns and prayers.

For a simple example of this latter practice, we may take the ancient ordination prayer for a bishop found in one form or another in virtually every Eastern Christian tradition. It includes a phrase from Romans 2:19-20, "a guide to the blind, a light to those who are in darkness, a corrector of the foolish, a teacher of children." In its original context the quotation has no connection at all with ordination or ministry. Instead, it is part of a passage directed toward Paul's Jewish contemporaries, whom he criticizes for being sure that they were all these things, because they were instructed in the Law; he believes that, in their efforts to teach others, they had failed to teach themselves. In the prayer, however, it has entirely lost both the association with the Jews and also the ironical tone of its original setting, and become simply a part of a list of qualities being sought from God for the new bishop.

Similarly, before the advent of modern biblical scholarship, Christians were willing to see almost unlimited allegorical or typological connections between images and incidents in the Old Testament and passages in the New, and also between those scriptural texts and the particular occasion being celebrated liturgically. While some of these applications may still be accepted as legitimate today, others on the contrary appear very strained and artificial to modern eyes. We have already seen in the previous chapter one example of this sort of excess in the extension of a christological interpretation to all of the psalms. Many scholars today would argue that such uses not only do violence to the original sense of texts by not seeing them within their own historical and cultural setting as understood by modern biblical criticism, but also fail to take into account the enormous changes in theological perspective and overall vision of the world that have taken place in our post-Enlightenment age, and resort instead to a quasi fundamentalist interpretation of the scriptures.

We argued in the previous chapter that authorial intent is not necessarily determinative of the interpretation of a biblical text, but that multiple meanings are possible. If this is true, it does not eliminate the possibility of such things as a typological use of scripture in worship or the appropriation of biblical phrases and images in Christian liturgical texts. It merely requires that we exercise greater care and critical acumen when we are either continuing past practices or creating new selections. We should also bear in mind that there are clear signs that a number of the psalms and other biblical books are themselves composite creations, the result of bringing together two or more pre-existent separate units. There is therefore nothing inherently foreign to their character in dividing them once again into their constituent parts for use in worship.

Thus, didactic and anamnetic ministries of the Word fulfill essentially complementary roles. The one enables scripture to be seen as a whole and sets individual passages within a larger context with opportunity for reflection and application of the text to diverse situations and individual needs. The other focuses attention upon particularly significant portions, relating them closely to the worship life of the church and using their proclamation to stimulate and enhance the corporate response to God's self revelation.

Suggestions for Further Reading

Bradshaw, Paul F. "The Use of the Bible in Liturgy: Some Historical Perspectives," *Studia Liturgica* 22 (1992): 35-52.

Old, Hughes Oliphant. *The Reading and Preaching of the Scriptures in the Worship of the Christian Church.* 3 volumes, Grand Rapids: Eerdmans, 1998-1999.

Schüssler Fiorenza, Elisabeth. "'For the Sake of Our Salvation': Biblical Interpretation and the Community of Faith," in *Bread Not Stone: The Challenge of Feminist Biblical Interpretation.* Boston: Beacon Press, 1984. Pp. 23-42.

7

WORDS AND ACTIONS

Most books about prayer, even liturgical prayer, concentrate on the words of prayer—and so far this one has been no exception to the rule. Yet it is vitally important to recognize that one of the things that distinguishes "cathedral" from "monastic" prayer is that it involves not just the mind and the voice but the whole body. As we have already indicated, while some forms of "monastic" prayer may include directions about posture and other outward gestures, these are never considered to belong to the essence of that prayer; they are merely aids to its practice, and may ultimately be dispensed with, since it is the interior activity that constitutes the true heart of the prayer. In "cathedral" prayer, on the other hand, the externals are just as important as the inner disposition, and belong to its very nature.

We shall now survey some of the main actions that accompanied the words of such prayer in the early history of Christianity. The intention behind this is certainly not to engage in a form of "liturgical fundamentalism," that is, it is not meant to imply that we ought to imitate exactly what the early Christians did simply because they did it. Its purpose is rather to remind ourselves of the importance that was attached to these externals at that formative period of Christian history, and to ask ourselves why it is that we so rarely embody our prayer in similar actions today. If the answer to this question turns out to be that we see no need to do so, that these are just optional extras for those who like that sort of thing, then this will serve as a useful barometer to indicate how far all our praying has moved in the direction of a "monastic" concept of prayer, even if at a conscious level we might claim otherwise.

On the other hand, we may be tempted to answer that bothering about such things as the right posture or precise direction for praying belongs to a primitive approach to religion, which more sophisticated Christians have outgrown, or conveys a concept of God that we would want to disavow. Surely, we may say, God does not care which way we face as long as we do actually pray? But it is not a question of religious law, of whether God wants certain actions performed—no early Christian went so far as to claim that—but of the appropriate form of human response to God. Prayer that is divorced from ritual action does not involve the whole person; it is in effect a form of dualism, which denies to our physical bodies any great importance in the worship of God. Alternatively, for some people, reluctance to engage in ritual acts may be based on a fear of falling into a mechanistic attitude toward worship, in which the external actions alone suffice, without reference to the interior disposition. But distorting prayer in one direction in order to escape the risk of the opposite distortion hardly seems a balanced approach.

It may even be that all the reasons that we might advance for dispensing with externals are not the true heart of the matter, but that our protests really stem from sheer embarrassment at being asked to make any public expression of our private piety. Christians of the present day are often uncomfortable with performing rituals that previous generations of believers took for granted, not because we reject ritual itself—after all, our everyday, secular lives are full of rituals with which we feel perfectly at home—but because we do not want other people to know that we take our faith and our prayer life that seriously. The result of this, of course, is that we lose a valuable opportunity to witness to an unbelieving world. Our faith is made invisible to others, in sharp contrast to devout Moslems, for example, who not only stop whatever they are doing to pray five times each day, but take care to face Mecca and prostrate themselves, no matter where they may happen to be, and even carry with them prayer mats for use at these times.

Beginnings

When we pray, most of us just begin. We do not employ rituals that mark out the time and space of prayer from the rest of life and so help us cross the threshold from everyday living to the holy. Instead, we simply launch right into the words. Early Christians, however, acted differently. They would first wash their hands and make the sign of the cross. The act of ritual purification with water has its roots in Jewish practice, where it was extended from the Temple cult to ordinary daily life both by the Essenes and by the Pharisees, and the outward washing symbolized the inner purity desired by the participants.

Only remnants of this once universal custom of washing the hands before prayer remain in contemporary Christian practice, although the same ritual is widespread in non-Christian religions of the East. Roman Catholic churches customarily have holy water containers situated next to the entrances, in which worshippers may dip their fingers as they pass. Most Roman Catholics are accustomed to do this not only upon entering but also on their way out of church, tracing the sign of the cross on themselves with their wet fingers, and understanding it as a ritual of blessing or warding off the powers of evil as they enter a holy place and as they go out into the world. Originally, however, it was only meant to be done as worshippers arrived to pray, so as to prepare them for this act, and its current form is obviously the result of the combination of what were originally two separate ritual acts—the handwashing and the sign of the cross.

Another remnant of the practice still found in some churches is the custom often known as the *lavabo*, when the presiding minister at a celebration of the Eucharist washes his or her hands just before beginning the eucharistic prayer. Many members of congregations imagine that this has something to do with hygiene—that the hands need to be clean before touching the eucharistic bread. But they miss the point: the action is not utilitarian but symbolic, and it comes at this point not because the presiding minister is about to touch the bread (indeed, in some ecclesiastical traditions he/she will already have handled the bread before this ceremony takes place), but because in the ancient church the presiding minister was about to proclaim the only prayer that he would say in the entire rite, and so naturally washed his hands before praying.

Orientation

Once again, most of us do not give a moment's thought as to the direction in which we should face to pray. But for early Christians, this too was important, and whenever possible they faced east for their prayers, whether they were joining with others in a formal service or saying daily prayers alone. The stress laid upon the direction even for individual praying is evident in this extract from a treatise on prayer written by the third-century theologian Origen, where he responds to those who apparently suggest that a beautiful view might be more appropriate for prayer, regardless of its direction:

> Now also we must say a few things about the region towards which we must look when praying. There being four regions, towards north and south, towards sunsetting and sunrising, who would not at once agree that the region towards the sunrising clearly indicates that we ought to make our prayers facing in that direction in symbolic fashion as though the soul beheld the rising of the true light? But since the door of the house may face in any direction, if a man desires to make his intercessions rather in the direction that the house opens, on the plea that the sight of heaven has something more inviting about it than looking at the wall, if the doors of the house happen not to look towards the sunrising, we must say to him that since it is by arrangement that the buildings of men open towards this or that region, while it is by nature that the east is preferred before the other regions, we must put that which is by nature before that which is by arrangement (*De or.* 32; English translation from E. G. Jay, *Origen's Treatise on Prayer* [London: SPCK, 1954], pp. 215-16)

Origen's reference to the symbolism of the eastward orientation— "as though the soul beheld the rising of the true light"—offers a clue to the source of this choice of direction. It was apparently a part of the eschatological vigilance of the early Christians, who expected the return of Christ to come from the east and so watched for that as they prayed. They seem to have inherited the custom from the Jewish Essenes, who also prayed facing the east as part of their eschatological hope. Of course, as time went by, the expectation of an immediate return of Jesus faded, and the eastward orientation then became instead one of the characteristics of Christian piety which marked them out from others—from Jews who faced Jerusalem to pray, and from Moslems who faced Mecca.

Posture

Recent years have seen an increasingly common custom among Christians of sitting for prayer—or rather of not moving from an existing sedentary position when beginning to pray, for it is not so much a matter of the deliberate choice of that posture for prayer as of not bothering to change posture at all in order to pray. Even those whose ecclesiastical tradition still normally expects them either to stand or to kneel in church will very often remain seated to pray in other contexts, as for example at grace before meals, when asked to join in prayer at a meeting of Christians, or in an informal prayer group. As far as this group of people is concerned, the roots of the custom appear to lie in the house masses and house prayer groups of the 1960s, when both the lack of physical space and the embarrassment felt at doing liturgical actions in an unconventional setting seemed to discourage movement from the chairs in which participants were sitting at the beginning of the rite. That this posture now tends to be treated as normal in all sorts of contexts is yet another sign of the prevailing conviction that externals are ultimately unimportant in worship; it is the inner spirit alone that matters.

All of this is in sharp contrast to the major part of Christian history to date, in which either standing or kneeling were the generally accepted positions for prayer, and in which posture mattered greatly, not only in public worship but also in private devotions too: for example, many adults of today can still remember being taught as children not just to pray before going to sleep but to *kneel* for prayer beside their beds.

At the same time, there is strong pressure from liturgical enthusiasts to make congregations stand up for most or all of the prayers at a celebration of the Eucharist, on the grounds that it is "what the early church did," with the implication that kneeling was a later and hence somewhat undesirable development. But that is not quite an accurate presentation of the facts. It was not so much that the early Christians stood for the celebration of the Eucharist as that they stood for worship on Sundays and during the fifty days of the Easter season, and that those were the only days on which the Eucharist was generally celebrated, at least until the second half of the fourth century. In other words, it was not so much the rite that was being marked in this way as the day. By applying the idea indiscriminately to all celebrations of the Eucharist, and sometimes to other worship services as well, regardless of the day on which they are being held, our liturgical enthusiasts are actually contributing, albeit unintentionally, to an indifference concerning liturgical time, which is as equally an important aspect of the externals of worship as is posture.

Early Christians not only stood or knelt for prayer, according to the day of the week, but also assumed what is called the *orant* position for their prayers—that is, they raised their hands upwards, following Jewish precedent (see, for example, Psalms 134:2; 141:2; 1 Timothy 2:8). This gesture, however, was soon transformed into a stretching out of the hands in symbolic representation of the crucifixion, and then eventually abandoned by all except the presiding minister at public worship, who continued to adopt it when reciting prayers as representative of the congregation. Ordinary Christians substituted instead the less public and dramatic gesture of joining the hands together when they were saying their own prayers, although in recent years this too has tended to disappear from use. On the other hand, those involved in the charismatic movement have now begun to restore the more expressive *orant* gesture to their worship.

While ancient Christian writers laid great stress on the importance in prayer of conforming physical action to word, they were nevertheless not insensitive to the fact that there were situations where this was simply not possible, either because of some physical disability afflicting individual worshippers or because the location in which worshippers found themselves did not permit it. Once again, Origen deals with the problem:

> These things I assert must be particularly observed, apart
> from any adverse circumstance; for when there is an adverse
> circumstance, it is fitting that permission be given sometimes
> to pray sitting because of some disease of the feet which
> cannot be regarded lightly, or even lying down because of
> fevers or such sicknesses; and in some circumstances, for
> example if we are on a voyage, or business does not allow us to
> return to fulfil our obligation of prayer, it is possible to pray

without attempting to do this. (*De or.* 31; in Jay, *Origen's Treatise on Prayer*, p. 210)

Such provisions were obviously intended to be the exception rather than the rule. Yet the opposite is more often the case today.

OTHER CEREMONIES

In addition to the disposition of the body, early Christians also included other ceremonies in their daily prayers. The account of evening prayer at Jerusalem written by Egeria, which we quoted in the first chapter, lays considerable stress upon the brightness of the lights at that service. As we said there, this was not something unique to the place, but a ritual lighting of the lamps was an important part of evening worship in many parts of the fourth-century church. Whether influenced by the Jewish lighting of the sabbath lamp or by similar light rituals among contemporary pagan cults in the Mediterranean region, Christian communities, assembled for prayer as darkness fell, would light the lamps and give thanks to God for the gift of the natural light of the day which they had enjoyed, for the gift of lamplight to scatter the darkness and terror of the night, and for the gift of the light of the world, Jesus Christ. Often the hymn *Phos hilaron*, "O Gladsome Light," still used in worship by many Christians today, was sung at this moment.

Here we see another close association between words and actions, and again one which did not belong exclusively to corporate worship but could also be part of an individual's prayer. This is revealed most clearly to us in a very touching account written by Gregory of Nyssa of a visit to his sister Macrina in 379 as she lay dying:

> Meanwhile evening had come and a lamp was brought in. All at once she opened the orb of her eyes and looked towards the light, clearly wanting to repeat the thanksgiving sung at the Lighting of the Lamps. But her voice failed and she fulfilled her intention in the heart and by moving her hands, and her lips moved in sympathy with her inward desire. But when she had finished the thanksgiving, and her hand brought to her face to make the Sign [of the cross] had signified the end of the prayer, she drew a great deep breath and closed her life

and her prayer together. (*Life of St Macrina* 25; English
translation from W.K. Lowther Clarke, *St. Gregory of Nyssa,
The Life of St. Macrina* [London: SPCK, 1916] p. 57)

Although such a ritual does not perhaps have the same power for
twentieth-century Westerners, accustomed to the provision of light at
the touch of a switch, as it did for people of previous ages and in other
cultures, there are clear signs that wherever light ceremonies have been
reintroduced into Christian worship in recent years, they have proved
very popular, seeming somehow to touch some subconscious primitive response to this primal element.

Lamplighting was not the only ceremonial accompaniment to
early Christian prayer. The first indication of the Christian use of incense occurs in Egeria's account of worship at Jerusalem in the late
fourth century, where it apparently was restricted to one weekly service alone, the early morning Sunday vigil commemorating the resurrection of Christ. Why it should have been associated with this occasion and no other at this time is not clear; the suggestion that it was
meant to represent the spices that the women brought to the tomb on
Easter morning (Mark 16:1; Luke 24:1) is not entirely convincing, and
sounds more like a later rationalization of the practice than its root
cause.

Yet whatever the origin of that particular custom, from the fifth
century onwards the offering of incense became a regular feature of
daily morning and evening worship in many places. This development
is not hard to explain. Already in the fourth century morning and
evening prayer were beginning to be thought of as the true fulfillment
of the daily morning and evening sacrifices of ancient Israel. Now, one
of the daily offerings prescribed in the Old Testament was incense:
"Aaron shall offer fragrant incense on [the altar]; every morning when
he dresses the lamps he shall burn it, and when Aaron sets up the
lamps in the evening, he shall offer it, a regular incense offering before
the LORD" (Exodus 30:7-8). Moreover, Psalm 141, with a reference to
incense in verse 2, rapidly became a standard element of evening prayer
in many places: "Let my prayer be counted as incense before you, and
the lifting up of my hands as an evening sacrifice." It was but a small
step, therefore, to match action to words and concepts, and introduce
a literal offering of incense in morning and evening worship. It did not
take place earlier than this chiefly because it had such painful associa-

tions for Christians before the fourth century: during periods of persecution they had been pressured by the pagan authorities to deny their faith by offering incense to the emperor as a god.

In some cases the incense was understood as symbolizing the prayers of the saints rising up to heaven, an idea that was already present in Christian circles in New Testament times, as the vision of the worship of heaven in Revelation 8:3-4 testifies:

> Another angel with a golden censer came and stood at the
> altar; he was given a great quantity of incense to offer with the
> prayers of all the saints on the golden altar that is before the
> throne. And the smoke of the incense, with the prayers of the
> saints, rose before God from the hand of the angel.

In other cases, the incense was understood as being an expiatory offering for sin, an interpretation derived from its use in this way in the Old Testament: "Moses said to Aaron, 'Take your censer, and put fire therein from off the altar and lay incense on it, and carry it quickly to the congregation and make atonement for them'" (Numbers 16:46).

ENDINGS

Just as important as beginnings for the act of prayer are endings. We do not know of any special ritual linked to the conclusion of a period of individual prayer among the early Christians, but it is clear that the end of prayer in communal settings was firmly marked with symbolic action. The earliest sources tell of the use of a kiss between participants functioning as "the seal of prayer" both in more public services and also between family members at home (see Tertullian, *De or.* 18; Clement, *Paed.* 3.12; Origen, *Comm. in Rom.* 10.33). In order to appreciate the significance of this act, we need to be aware of its counter-cultural impact: in the pagan world which surrounded the early Christians, kissing was a sign of intimacy and was thus restricted to close blood relatives, friends of the same sex, and one's spouse. Therefore, for the Christian community to share a kiss on the mouth (for that is how it was done) with one another, in most cases regardless of gender, was a vivid expression of their intimate union in the body of Christ and of the concerted nature of their prayer, although it was regarded by those outside as a scandal and a sign of the Christians' libertinism.

The custom of concluding prayer with a kiss continued to be a part of later Christian rites, although often understood in a somewhat different sense. In the Eucharist, it was commonly viewed as an expression of reconciliation in preparation for the eucharistic action that was to follow it rather than as the seal of the prayers of the faithful that had preceded it; in Baptism, as a gesture of welcome toward the newly initiated members; and in ordination, as a sign of acceptance into the collegial fellowship of the ordained ministry.

However, in the case of daily acts of worship, the kiss disappeared and was replaced in the fourth century by a different concluding rite with a slightly different emphasis. Egeria tells us that at the end of each service the faithful went up to the hand of the bishop to receive an individual blessing, and her information is confirmed by other sources. This dismissal rite was called in Latin *missa*, and eventually gave its name to any liturgical unit within a rite, and ultimately to a rite as a whole, which is how the Eucharist in the West came to be known as the Mass. This development in the meaning of the word might seem rather strange at first sight—Why should the final moments of a rite become the name for the whole thing?—until we reflect on how lengthy such a dismissal process would have been. For each person to go up to the bishop and receive an individual laying on of hands and blessing must have occupied a considerable proportion of the total time given over to the prayer service. In other words, it was not really the equivalent of the modern dismissal at the end of the service, but something closer to the greeting of each member of the congregation by the minister at the church door after the service. That early Christians were prepared to accord the dismissal so much time within each service every day is an indication of the degree of importance that they attached to it. But we should also note that the transformation of a kiss into a laying on of hands marks a shift in the concept of the church—from a gathering of equals who greet one another to a more hierarchical model in which people are joined together by their association with the bishop. Eventually, this latter practice did come to be thought of as too time-consuming, and was replaced by a blessing pronounced over the entire congregation collectively.

SUGGESTIONS FOR FURTHER READING

Fischer, Balthasar. *Signs, Words, and Gestures*. New York: Pueblo Publishing Company, 1981.

Grimes, Ronald. *Reading, Writing, and Ritualizing*. Washington, D.C.: Pastoral Press, 1993.

Imber Black, Evan, and Janine Roberts. *Rituals for Our Times*. New York: HarperCollins, 1992.

Northup, Lesley A. *Ritualizing Women*. Cleveland, Ohio: Pilgrim Press, 1997.

Pottebaum, Gerard A. *The Rites of People: Exploring the Ritual Character of Human Experience*. Rev. ed. Washington D.C.: Pastoral Press, 1992.

8

Patterns of Daily Prayer

As has been stressed in earlier chapters, the distinction between "cathedral" and "monastic" ways of praying can be applied not just to the practice of daily prayer but to all acts of worship, including the celebration of the Eucharist or of other sacramental rites. Nevertheless, the distinction obviously has particular implications for the choice of a pattern of daily prayer that Christians might follow.

We have also seen in earlier chapters that "cathedral" and "monastic" should be distinguished from each other not by merely looking at the outward form of prayer but primarily by what praying people think that they are doing: an apparently "monastic" form may in reality be prayed with a "cathedral" intention, and conversely a "cathedral" form may be used for a "monastic" way of praying. Thus, it is certainly possible to employ almost any pattern of prayer for either purpose, and we do not switch from one style of praying to the other merely by putting an end to a *cursus* of psalmody, reducing the quantity of scripture read in the service, and making sure that certain elements feature in it, as for example Psalm 141 in the evening office.

This suggests that what we most need in order to promote "cathedral" prayer alongside the "monastic" character of our devotions is not so much a change in external forms as a renewal of our spirituality. On the other hand, it is unlikely that such a transformation of spirituality will be brought about unless at the same time some modification of the forms themselves occurs. The recent revision of eucharistic rites in many Christian traditions provides a parallel here. What was of greatest importance with regard to the eucharist was not the replacement of traditional orders of service with ones that better reflected the shape of the primitive rite, but the effecting of a transformation in the way in which people envisaged and participated in eucharistic worship itself. The advocates of the twentieth-century liturgical movement first struggled to do this at a time when there was no prospect of official liturgical revision taking place, but found that they could succeed only up to a point. Their efforts were resisted by the rites themselves with all the connotations that traditionally attached to them. It was only when the text and rubrics were changed that it really become possible to engender a new eucharistic theology and spirituality.

Thus it is a great deal easier to pray—and to help others to learn to pray—if the form reflects the particular function intended, and if we are not forced to engage in a type of ecclesiastical double-speak which requires that, when reciting a psalm that asks for the destruction of our enemies, we justify it on the grounds that what we are really doing is interceding on their behalf. Without wanting to detract at all, therefore, from the importance of the process of formation in the spirituality of liturgical praying that must accompany any revision of forms if they are to have any chance of becoming what their compilers intend, the remainder of this chapter will be given over to a consideration of appropriate forms of daily prayer.

Recent volumes containing material for daily prayer, whether official publications of ecclesiastical bodies or private compilations by individuals, have rarely reflected the vision of "cathedral" prayer that this book has tried to articulate. Some of them have been unequivocally "monastic" in their approach, for example, offering spiritual reading for reflection and meditation together with prayers for personal growth. Others have been but simplified and modified versions of the traditional forms of daily office from their own denomination, or borrowings of some such form from another church. Some of these, while claiming to have restored a more "cathedral" style of worship, have at the same time often added directives encouraging periods of silence to be kept after psalms and readings, effectively bringing into the rite a stronger "monastic" dimension. All in all, confusion seems more evident than clarity of purpose. How is the disciplined, praying Christian to choose?

For example, the Roman Catholic Liturgy of the Hours, as the daily office is now called in that tradition, has basically slimmed down—but not radically disturbed—the classical Benedictine and Roman structure of each of the canonical hours of prayer. Morning and evening prayer, for instance, like their traditional counterparts, are still principally composed of introductory responses, a hymn, a block of psalms, a short reading, a responsory, a gospel canticle, and prayers. The psalms may be fewer in number, with the cycle of psalmody being spread over four weeks instead of just one, and the hymn may be in a different position, but there has apparently been no major reconsideration of the function that those hours are intended to fulfill or of the design of an appropriate form to give adequate expression to that function.

Similarly, the recitation of the psalter in essentially its biblical order and the reading of the other books of the Bible in a consecutive manner still form the nucleus of nearly all recent revisions of the daily office throughout the Anglican Communion. The burden of the heavy scriptural diet may have been lightened by spreading both the psalmody and lections more thinly over a longer period of time, and the fare may have been rendered a little less monotonous by the provision of different canticles for each day of the week and a wider selection of other seasonal material, but this amounts only to the sugar coating of a bitter pill. The symptoms of spiritual indigestion have been treated, but the root cause of the condition still remains, for the basic structure and spirituality of the traditional forms have not been fundamentally disturbed.

THE HEART OF "CATHEDRAL" PRAYER

As we have seen earlier, there are two primary constituents of a "cathedral" pattern of prayer—praise and intercession. Those who are responsible for drawing up such forms of worship today might well choose to express the element of praise either by means of some of the canonical psalms and canticles that are strongly laudatory in character or by means of nonbiblical poems or hymns, whether ancient or modern, or through some combination of any of these. The provision of a form of intercession presents rather more difficulty. On the one hand, it needs to contain sufficient freedom and flexibility to enable specific local and current concerns to be inserted within the petitions and so avoid the prayer descending to the level of banal generalities that do not capture the minds and hearts of the worshippers ("O God, bless everyone"). On the other hand, it needs to provide sufficient structure and precision both to prevent the activity from being converted into a time of introverted reflection and meditation and also to direct the prayer beyond the merely personal and immediate subjects that come to mind and toward the less obvious and more wide ranging responsibilities of the church in relation to the world.

While classical forms of the "cathedral" office did not generally include any scriptural readings at all, this does not mean that "cathedral" prayer must never have any readings attached to it. As we have suggested in a previous chapter, the verses of the psalms generally functioned there as a form of ministry of the Word, to which the communal refrain was a response. Furthermore, it might be said that both the praise and intercession were responses to an unspoken proclamation of God's gracious actions in the world. Therefore, the addition of an anamnetic ministry of the Word can be understood as a making explicit what was implicit in that worship and so as an enrichment of it. Since proclamation precedes response, the logical position for such an element in the sequence of the rite would be immediately before the praise and intercession.

As the previous chapter argued, attention to beginnings and endings is also important in shaping a form of prayer. The beginning of evening prayer might well include the lighting of a candle and thanksgiving for daylight/lamplight/the light of Christ. Excellent forms of this for the various seasons of the year can be found in *Praise God in Song* (see the end of the chapter for publication details). For morning prayer, an appropriate equivalent is not so obvious in the tradition, but a form of thanksgiving for creation/resurrection/rebirth through baptism, accompanied by sprinkling with water would be one possibility.

THE COMBINATION OF "MONASTIC" AND "CATHEDRAL" ELEMENTS

As we observed at the beginning of this book, many forms of worship throughout history have included both "cathedral" and "monastic" elements within the same service, and so there is nothing inherently difficult about doing this in a modern pattern of daily prayer.

For instance, one or more biblical readings followed by a homily, silent reflection, or group discussion could precede the core of praise and intercession of "cathedral" prayer. I have included in an appendix to this book just one example among many of the ways that this combination can be effected. This particular example comes from the 1989 *United Methodist Hymnal*. Here the nucleus is clearly "cathedral" in character with more "monastic" additions enclosed within brackets as an optional extension to the celebration.

However, such a pattern is not without danger. Because the "monastic" element of the worship will often occupy more time and more readily feed the spiritual hunger of the individual than the "cathedral" element that follows it, it is all too easy for it to be thought of as the heart and prime purpose of the time of prayer, with the praise and intercession as no more than a conclusion to it, and one which moreover will tend to become interpreted in the light of what has preceded: the praise will be seen as praise for what God has done for me, the intercession as prayer for my needs, and the vision of the praise and prayer of the church for the world will quickly be lost. It may therefore often be preferable to keep the two types of prayer quite separate in time, or at least to ensure that the "cathedral" worship comes first, with the "monastic" prayer perhaps taking place in a different location afterward, to emphasize the different, though complementary, character of the two activities.

THE QUESTION OF PSALMODY

The use of psalms within a pattern of daily prayer calls for a special word. We have suggested in chapter 5 that they may be employed in a number of quite different roles—as hymns of praise, as prayers, as christological poems, or as scriptural lections—depending upon their particular character. But it is essential that these distinct functions are effectively communicated to those asked to use the psalms. It is no good the leaders of worship knowing that the first psalm in a service is meant to be seen God's word to us and the second as our hymn of praise to God, if the congregation still think of both psalms as two similar liturgical compositions, and have no idea why they are saying or singing either of them at all. Effective communication can be achieved in part by more teaching about the psalms, but it also depends to a great extent on paying much more attention to how psalms are performed than people commonly do.

Decisions about the way psalms are to be said or sung (antiphonally, responsorially, etc.) are usually made without reference to the nature and contents of the particular psalm itself, and often on the basis of a mere desire for variation or some purely musical consideration: "We did the first psalm responsorially, so let's do the second one antiphonally; we need variety so that the choir doesn't get bored." While it is true that varied methods of performing the psalms first made an appearance in early monasticism precisely in order to relieve the tedium of the labor of chanting them, that does not prevent twentieth-century Christians from taking a more reasoned approach to the issue. One of the best ways of helping people to understand what they are doing when using a psalm is to arrange its performance in such a way as to bring out its meaning.

If we consider first the distinction between psalms that we see as God's word to us and psalms that we see as our words to God, it is obviously going to be very hard for people to understand a psalm as addressed to us if we all recite it together in unison, or even if one half of the congregation does the odd numbered verses and the other side the even numbered ones. Surely, such a psalm calls out for a solo voice to which the others listen. When used in "monastic" prayer, it may be read meditatively, with perhaps a considerable period of silence between each verse, and an appropriate collect at the end; when used in "cathedral" prayer, it may be sung responsorially, with an suitable refrain after each verse; but in either case the important thing is for the congregation to understand that they are to listen to what is being said to them. It may also be a help in making this distinction between the different functions of psalms if we ask people to sit for this type of psalm and conversely to stand in order to say or sing psalms that are intended as our words to God. After all, the tradition of sitting for psalms originated in early monasticism when psalms were understood as God's word to us.

We also need to take into greater consideration the contents of each psalm. If a psalm is very lengthy, it may call for several lectors or cantors to be used in succession for different sections of the psalm in order to sustain interest. If the psalm itself has different voices within it, then it really demands that different people say or sing those parts in order to communicate its meaning, which remains hidden when every verse is performed in exactly the same way. Similarly, different parts of a psalm may require quite different treatment from one another, as the character of the text changes.

Above all, one of the most crucial elements in an intelligent approach to psalmody is the choice and use of refrains or responses. Some psalms already have a refrain built in to them, so why add another? In Psalm 136, for instance ("O give thanks to the LORD for he is good, for his steadfast love endures for ever"), every one of the twenty six verses has the same second half: "for his steadfast love endures for ever." It makes no sense at all to perform this psalm by alternating verses, whether between one half of the congregation and the other or between leader and congregation. Nor does it need a response added to it. The psalm is crying out to be divided by half verses, with a leader saying or singing the first half of each verse, and the congregation responding with the second half. Or again, Psalm 24 ("The earth is the LORD's and all that is in it") changes its character dramatically from verse 7 onward, and engages in a dialogue: "Lift up your heads, O gates! and be lifted up, O ancient doors! that the King of glory may come in." The question is then asked; "Who is the King of glory?" And the response comes: "The LORD, strong and mighty, the LORD, mighty in battle," followed again by the appeal, "Lift up your heads, O gates! and be lifted up, O ancient doors! that the King of glory may come in," and so on. Surely, such psalms as this need to be performed in a way that will bring out this dialogic form.

These examples also serve to remind us that we do not have to put a refrain automatically after every verse, or even after every second or third verse; indeed such a mechanical and insensitive approach to a psalm text can be destructive of its meaning. We need to insert a refrain only where it makes sense. And most importantly of all, we need to choose an appropriate refrain. Let us not automatically pick the first verse as the refrain, regardless of what it says, as though any verse would do, no matter what its content. Nor need we insist that the refrain has to be taken out of the particular psalm that we are using. Why not a verse from another psalm, or even from somewhere else in scripture, if that helps to make the best sense for the psalm in its particular context? For while it is true that the earliest Christian practice was to use only verses from the psalm, later tradition was more adventurous, and even went as far as using nonscriptural texts. There is no reason why we must always conclude that the early church was better than the later church: not all developments have been for the worse rather than the better.

Perhaps the importance of choosing appropriate refrains can best be illustrated by considering the use of Psalm 22 during Holy Week. The first verse of the psalm ("My God, my God, why have you forsaken me?") is often used as the response, thereby encouraging the congregation to identify themselves with the subject of the psalm, whereas traditionally this psalm has been interpreted as the words of Christ. After all, according to Mark's Gospel, this verse was on the lips of the dying Jesus. Surely at this time we want people to think about the suffering that Jesus underwent for us and our salvation. It is hardly appropriate, therefore, to encourage them to identify themselves with Jesus, to suggest that the minor discomforts of the suburban lives of many of us in any way compare with the pain and dereliction endured by our Savior. Would it not be better to find a response for this season that enabled the assembly to express its reverence for what Christ has done? Two possible alternatives come to mind: "Christ Jesus became obedient unto death, even death on a cross," echoing Philippians 2:8, and "By his wounds, we are healed" (Isaiah 53:5). Both of these are drawn from passages often read in this week and seem to capture the desired attitude much better, thus helping people to hear the psalm itself as the words of Christ to which they are asked to respond.

TIMES AND SEASONS

Although morning and evening have tended to become generally accepted as the most appropriate times for prayer, they do not always fit comfortably with the demands of everyone's life. For some, it may be more practical to gather with other Christians at midday, during a lunch break at the office or factory for example, than at the beginning or end of the day; for shift workers or students in colleges, some other hour may be better; and so on. But it may not be the best solution for these varied needs to produce some generic form of prayer that will do for any hour of the day or night. One of the strengths of classical forms of the daily office is that they have incorporated material appropriate to the particular hour of its celebration. The traditional late evening monastic service of Compline, for example, has proved popular with many people in large part precisely because it addresses what are common human concerns at bedtime—the need to lay aside the worries of the day and to look for security during the hours of sleep.

Prayer thus ideally needs to be firmly rooted in time itself, to relate to the rhythm of the day and night, and to make remembrance of the biblical themes associated with particular moments of the day. By ancient tradition, for example, the ninth hour of the day (3:00 P.M.) has functioned as a memorial of the passion of Christ, and the third hour (9:00 A.M.) as a commemoration of the gift of the Holy Spirit (see Acts 2:15). When those themes are abstracted from that hour and celebrated at some other time of the day, they lose much of the force which that association gave to them. For the same reason, morning prayer has much less meaning as a celebration of the gift of the new day and a memorial of creation and resurrection if it takes place long after the day has begun; and evening prayer makes much less sense as a thanksgiving for the light of the day and for the light, both physical and spiritual, to guide us through the night if candles are lit and the office celebrated while there are several hours of daylight left and many more activities of the day still to pursue.

It is not only the hours of each day but the seasons of the liturgical year that can play a part in the Christian remembrance in prayer of God's actions toward humanity. For that reason, in formulating patterns of prayer for Christians to use, it is desirable not only to provide forms appropriate to different times of the day and night (even though all Christians will not attempt to pray at every one of them) but also to allow them to reflect the changing theological focus of the different parts of the church year. So often compilers introduce variations into patterns of daily prayer merely in order to prevent boredom arising through monotony, sometimes even without regard for the inappropriateness of different psalms or canticles to the days or times to which they are then allocated. It is greatly to be preferred that any such changes should mark significant points and shifts in liturgical time.

For example, it is much less important from a Christian point of view to differentiate Tuesday from Monday in a cycle of prayer than it is to mark out Sundays from the other days of the week (for example, by a resurrection reading and appropriate canticle), although there might be an argument for also giving Friday prayer a special character as a memorial of the passion of Christ. Similarly, unchanging forms of prayer throughout the fifty days of the Easter might have a significant value in conveying the liturgical unity of that season, and in any case ought to have a very different style from prayer during Lent (which might, for instance, begin each day with Psalm 51).

COMMUNAL AND INDIVIDUAL

The prayer of the church does not require that every individual member must necessarily participate at every prescribed hour of prayer, whether with others or alone. Even in the early centuries of Christianity, when bishops were pressing the clergy and people to add to their daily cycle all the hours of prayer then being observed in monastic communities, it was the common custom for different churches in a city to take responsibility for one particular hour of the day, thus sharing the duty between them. Something similar may well be appropriate for Christian congregations today. Different groups and organizations in a parish, for example, may take upon themselves the responsibility for celebrating evening prayer in the church on one evening of the week, and so on. Similarly, those who through sickness, age, or disability are house-bound can be invited to play their part in the church's prayer by assuming responsibility for those hours at which others are not easily available. In this way, the whole congregation may be assigned a ministry at different times and to different degrees in the unceasing praise and intercession of God's people

The effective implementation of such a pattern, however, presents certain requirements to those responsible for drawing up orders of daily prayer: the format must be easily understood and simple to use if it is to commend itself to ordinary churchgoers; rubrics must be flexible enough to cater for a wide variety of different situations, but at the same time should encourage a true liturgical celebration, where possible, involving movement and ceremonial and not merely a sedentary recitation; and texts should include musical settings simple enough to prompt singing in even the smallest of groups. On the other hand, we must not let the quite proper attention that we give to such details obscure the fundamental point that we have sought to make throughout this book, that the transformation of the prayer life of Christian people demands not just the change of external forms but a fundamental renewal of their inner spirituality, in which it is hoped that the contents of this book may be able to play some part.

SUGGESTIONS FOR FURTHER READING

Bradshaw, Paul F. "The Daily Office," in Michael Perham, ed. *Towards Liturgy 2000*. London: SPCK 1989. Pp. 27-33.

Melloh, John A. and William G. Storey, eds. *Praise God in Song: Ecumenical Daily Prayer*. Chicago: G.I.A. Publications, 1979.

Roberts, Paul; David Stancliffe; and Kenneth Stevenson, eds. *Something Understood*. London: Hodder & Stoughton, 1993.

Taft, Robert. F. "The Divine Office; Monastic Choir, Prayer Book, or Liturgy of the People of God? An Evaluation of the New Liturgy of the Hours in its Historical Context," in René Latourelle, ed. *Vatican II: Assessment and Perspectives*, volume 2. New York: Paulist Press, 1989. Pp. 27-46.

APPENDIX

From the earliest days of the church, Christian worshipers saw the rising of the sun and the lighting of the evening lamps as symbolic of Christ's victory over death. "An Order for Morning Praise and Prayer" and "An Order for Evening Praise and Prayer" enable Christians to celebrate daily the life, death, and resurrection of Jesus Christ.

These services focus upon the praise of God and prayer for God's creation rather than the proclaiming of the Word. Therefore, preaching or other devotional talks are inappropriate in these services. When Scripture is used, passages should be chosen that will encourage the community in its praise and prayer.

Each order reflects a simple yet flexible pattern. The openings, hymns, songs of praise, responses to prayers, and Lord's Prayer may all be sung, with or without accompaniment. Scripture, silence, and prayer are optional, as indicated by brackets.

Each order is to be celebrated in a community of Chris-tians at various occasions in their life together. These orders may be used on any occasion when Christians gather, but they are not adequate substitutes for the full Sunday Service of Word and Table.

Laity are encouraged to lead these services. Different parts of the service may be led by different people.

The communal quality of prayer is emphasized when the people stand or sit in a circle or other arrangement facing one another. There may be a simple setting with a focus such as a cross or candle.

Both orders of Praise and Prayer are adapted from The United Methodist Hymnal 1989, © The United Methodist Publishing House, 1989 and used by permission.

An Order for Morning Praise and Prayer

This service is for groups as they begin their day in prayer.

CALL TO PRAISE AND PRAYER *Sung or spoken:*

> O Lord, open our lips.
> **And we shall declare your praise.**

MORNING HYMN
A hymn appropriate to the morning may be sung.

PRAYER OF THANKSGIVING
The following or other prayer of thanksgiving may be said:

> New every morning is your love, great God of light,
> > and all day long you are working for good in the world.
> Stir up in us desire to serve you,
> > to live peacefully with our neighbors,
> > and to devote each day to your Son,
> > our Savior, Jesus Christ the Lord.
> > **Amen.**

SCRIPTURE
Psalm 51,63, or 95; Deuteronomy 6:4-9; Isaiah 55:1-3; John 1:1-5, 9-14; Romans 12:1-2; or other readings appropriate to the morning, or to the day or season of the Christian year, or to the nature of the occasion, may be used.

SILENCE
Silent meditation on the Scripture that has been read. This may be concluded with a short prayer.

SONG OF PRAISE
Psalm 100, 148, or 150; Canticle of God's Glory; Canticle of the Holy Trinity; Canticle of Light and Darkness; Canticle of Moses and Miriam;

Canticle of Praise to God; Canticle of Thanksgiving; Canticle of Zechariah; or other Scripture song or hymn may be sung.

Prayers of the People
The following or other litany of intercession may be prayed, during which any person may offer a brief prayer of intercession or petition.

After each prayer, the leader may conclude: Lord, in your mercy, *and all may respond:* **Hear our prayer.**

> Together, let us pray for
> > the people of this congregation . . . .
>
> > those who suffer and those in trouble . . . .
>
> > the concerns of this local community . . . .
>
> > the world, its people and its leaders . . . .
>
> > the church universal—its leaders, its members,
> > and its mission . . . .

Following these prayers, all may sing: "Hear Us, O God," "Jesus, Remember Me," "Let Us Pray to the Lord," "Remember Me," or "This Is Our Prayer."

The Lord's Prayer *Sung or spoken*

Blessing

> The grace of the Lord Jesus Christ,
> and the love of God,
> and the communion of the Holy Spirit
> be with you all.
> **Amen.**

The Peace
Signs of peace may be exchanged.

An Order for Evening Praise and Prayer

A candle may be lit and lifted in the midst of the community. The following may be sung or spoken:

> Light and peace in Jesus Christ.
> **Thanks be to God.**

Evening Hymn
"O Gladsome Light" or other hymn appropriate to the evening may be sung.

Prayer of Thanksgiving
The following or other prayer of thanksgiving may be said:

> We praise and thank you, O God,
>> for you are without beginning and without end.
> Through Christ, you created the whole world;
>> through Christ, you preserve it.
> You made the day for the works of light
>> and the night for the refreshment of
>>> our minds and our bodies.
> Keep us now in Christ; grant us a peaceful evening,
>> a night free from sin; and bring us at last to eternal life.
> Through Christ, and in the Holy Spirit,
>> we offer you all glory, honor, and worship,
>> now and for ever.
>> **Amen.**

Scripture
Psalm 23, 90, 121, 141; Genesis 1:1-5, 14-19; Exodus 13:21-22; Matthew 25:1-13; Romans 5:6-11; 1 Thessalonians 5:1-10; Revelation 22:1-5; or other readings appropriate to the evening, or to the day or season of the Christian year, or to the nature of the occasion, may be used.

Silence
Silent meditation on the Scripture that has been read. This may be concluded with a short prayer.

SONG OF PRAISE
Psalm 134, Canticle of Covenant Faithfulness, Canticle of Hope, Canticle of Light and Darkness, Canticle of Mary, Canticle of Simeon, or other Scripture song or hymn may be sung.

PRAYERS OF THE PEOPLE
The following or other litany of intercession may be prayed, during which any person may offer a brief prayer of intercession or petition.

After each prayer, the leader may conclude: Lord, in your mercy, *and all may respond:* **Hear our prayer.**

> Together, let us pray for
> > the people of this congregation . . . .
>
> > those who suffer and those in trouble . . . .
>
> > the concerns of this local community . . . .
>
> > the world, its people and its leaders . . . .
>
> > the church universal—its leaders, its members,
> > > and its mission . . . .
>
> > the communion of saints . . . .

Or, prayers of confession and words of pardon may be offered.

Following these prayers, all may sing: "Hear Us, o God," "Kyrie Eleison," "Lord, Have Mercy," or "Remember Me."

THE LORD'S PRAYER   *Sung or spoken*

BLESSING
> The grace of Jesus Christ enfold you this night.
> Go in peace.
> **Thanks be to God.**

THE PEACE
Signs of peace may be exchanged, or all may depart in silence.

93

ABBREVIATIONS

For those who are unfamiliar with the conventional abbreviations of the titles of patristic writings, the full versions of those cited in this book are given below, together with the relevant volume and column numbers of J.P. Migne's *Patrologia Graeca* [= PG] or *Patrologia Latina* [= PL] in which the text can be found. Most of them are also available in English translations.

Augustine, *Enarr. in Ps.* = *Enarrationes in Psalmos* ('Expositions of the Psalms"), PL 36-37
Basil, *Ep.* = *Epistolae* ("Letters"), PG 32:220-1112
Clement of Alexandria, *Paed.* = *Paedagogus* ("The Tutor"),
PG 8: 247-684
Strom. = *Stromata* ("Miscellanies"),
PG 8: 685-9:601
John Chrysostom, *Expos. in Ps.* = *Expositio in Psalmos* ("Explanation of the Psalms"), PG 55:35-528
Justin Martyr, *1 Apol.* = *Apologia prima* ("First Apology"), PG 6:328-440
Origen, *Comm. in Rom.* = *Commentaria in Epistolam ad Romanos* ("Commentary on the Epistle to the Romans"), PG 14:837-1292
De or. = *De oratione* ("On Prayer") PG 11:416-561
Socrates, *Hist. eccl.* = *Historia ecclesiastica* ("Ecclesiastical History"), PG 67:33-841
Tertullian, *Apol.* = *Apologeticus* ("Apology"), PL 1:305-604
De cult. fem. = *De cultu feminarum* ("On Women's Dress"),
PL 1:1417-1448
De ieiun. = *De ieiunio* ("On Fasting"), PL 2:953-978
De or. = *De oratione* ("On Prayer"), PL 1:1245-1304